The Shadow Dragon:

The Inside Story Behind Donald Trump's Struggle to Derail the Deep State Agenda

(patriot edition)

By Susan Bradford
(c) 2019

"When you open your heart to patriotism, there is no room for prejudice. The Bible tells us, 'How good it is when God's people live in unity'."

Donald J. Trump

"Rebellion to tyrants is obedience to God."

Thomas Jefferson

"Control the oil, and you control the nation."

Henry Kissinger

"I was very flattered when Henry Kissinger said I ran the State Department better than anybody had run it in a long time."

Hillary Clinton

"If the American people ever find out what we have done, they would chase us down the street and lynch us."

George H.W. Bush

"Our enemies never stop thinking of new ways to harm our country and our people, and neither do we."

George W. Bush

"Religion in America takes no direct part in the government in the government of society but nevertheless it must be regarded as the foremost of the political institutions of that country for if it does not impart a taste for freedom, it facilitates the use of free institutions."

Alexis de Tocqueville

"It is time to remember that old wisdom our soldiers will never forget: that whether we are black or brown or white, we all bleed the same red blood of patriots, we all enjoy the same glorious freedoms, and we all salute the same great American flag."

Donald J. Trump

Table of Contents

About the Author	**4**
The Advent of Fake News	**5**
The Backdoor of Socialism	**10**
Back Channels of the Deep State	**36**
Oil Diplomacy and Subversion	**61**
Treacherous Politicians	**86**
The Shadow Dragon	**118**
The Conquest of America	**123**
Trumping the Deep State	**145**
The Dragon Speaks	**150**

About the Author

Susan Bradford was the lead researcher in the Abramoff investigation who uncovered and methodically documented how Republican superlobbyist Jack Abramoff was set up for criminal prosecution by rival lobbyists who coveted his business in Indian Country. Over the course of her research, Susan uncovered the financial, intelligence, and political networks coursing through the nation's federally recognized Indian tribes which constitute the Deep State, as revealed in this book.

Susan holds a BA in English from UC Irvine and an MA in International Relations from the University of Essex. She has worn many hats within journalism, for example, as news production intern for CBS-TV news, news writer for KNX (CBS) news radio, assignments editor for the Voice of America, reporter and police bureau chief for City News Service, production assistant for the PBS Red Car Film Project, freelance producer for Fox News Channel, and founding editor of the *European Review*, the departmental publication for the Centre for European Studies at Essex University.

She has also served as speech writer for UK Shadow Foreign Secretary Michael Howard and Korean Ambassador Sung Chul Yang.

Susan has written many books, including, for example, *Lynched: The Shocking Story of How the Political Establishment Manufactured a Scandal to Have Republican Superlobbyist Jack Abramoff Removed from Power, The Full Court Press* (with Senior CBS Foreign Correspondent Tom Fenton), *The United Church of Heist,* and *The Tribes that Rockefeller Built*.

Her articles have appeared in the *European Review,* the *UN Vision,* the *Washington Times,* Capital Research Center's *Organizational Trends,* and elsewhere.

I.
The Advent of Fake News

After President Bill Clinton served two terms in office, a curious dynamic began unfolding across the United States. American news organizations were closing their foreign news bureaus *en masse*, citing limited financial resources, reduced advertising revenue, and a disengaged public. *The Columbia Journalism Review* noticed this worrying trend too, reporting that between 1998 and 2011, at least 20 media organizations had eliminated their foreign bureaus altogether.[i] Even more curious, the *CJR* observed, reporters with two prominent national broadsheets rarely left their offices to cover international stories, opting instead to aggregate and curate the work of others, many of whom had limited firsthand knowledge of what they were reporting. By 2012, seventy-five percent of the *Washington Post*'s foreign bureaus consisted of a single reporter.[ii] "Is the *Post* using the word 'bureau' a bit loosely," the *CJR* rightfully asked.

The cull of foreign correspondents didn't discriminate. Broadcast, print, and online media alike were cutting back on their coverage of international news. In the lead up to the War on Iraq, the nation witnessed one of the most shameful chapters in media history. The media did not serve as a check on power. Instead it drummed up support for the war without critically evaluating the merits of the intelligence reports used to justify invading and bombing another country. Reporters stumbled over themselves to report misinformation and serve as cheerleaders for war, allowing disastrous foreign policy to supersede national interest. The war proceeded unchallenged at a great cost to American blood and treasure.

The United States would never be the same after September 11, 2001. Instead of doubling down on their foreign coverage to help the public understand the world better, news organizations cut back their international coverage even further. Many journalists simply left the profession in frustration over their inability to do hard, objective reporting or to report stories honestly and within context. Journalists who attempted to be critical of those in power, beyond petulant snarky jabs, reported being silenced or retaliated against, at times losing their jobs. News was being spun in such a way as to advance a private agenda that the public knew little to nothing about.

More bloodletting followed, with many news organizations

issuing *mea culpas* once their flawed coverage of the Iraq War came to light. Instead of producing more hard hitting, investigative stories that served the public interest, the media descended into partisan warfare, with leftist pundits pillorying their conservative counterparts and vice-versa; their reporting did not educate the public but divided and destabilized the country further by filling the airways and broadsheets with toxic noise and obfuscation. While the American media once served the public interest, media executives claimed that they were simply delivering what the public wanted. Yet, the media continued to lose audience share and, by extension, advertising revenue.

If the media's coverage of the world and nation's capitol wasn't embarrassing enough, by 2016, the media had pronounced Democratic presidential candidate Hillary Clinton's imminent victory against her Republican challenger, Donald Trump, whose message and personal appeal filled amphitheaters and inspired many followers to don red Make America Great Again hats to demonstrate their support. Instead of carefully assessing the merits of the candidates' respective platforms to help the public make an informed decision in the election, the media dispensed with all objectivity and engaged in brazen, partisan cheer leading for Hillary while publicly defaming Trump and his followers as "racist, sexist, homophobic, Islamophobic xenophobes."

Trump won anyway much to the astonishment of the media, who should have been less astonished and more dedicated to uncovering and reporting the facts.

The media's credibility had fallen to an all time low, with YouTube stars like PewDiePie commanding vastly greater audience share than all the American television news networks and broadsheets combined. If news executives had rolled out their punch-throwing pundits to drive revenue, they had failed badly.

By not covering the news with rigor, thoughtfulness, objectivity, and context, the media had deliberately kept the American people uninformed and distracted.

The question was, why?

As foreign news coverage dissipated, the need for the American public to understand what was happening overseas was growing even greater.

By minimizing foreign news coverage, the media appeared to be deliberately hiding key information from the public while focusing on polarizing left-right debates and race baiting that divided the country further and led many to tune out the news altogether and disengage from politics out of disgust.

News organizations had closed their foreign bureaus precisely at the very point in which it was in the public's interest for them to be paying close attention.

While the media was busy denouncing the United States and keeping the public whipped up in an emotional frenzy, Communist China was rising as a powerful, threat that sought to usurp the role of the United States as global superpower.

The American people could complain about rising taxes, unaffordable housing, the exorbitant cost of educating their children, the disappearance of jobs and hard earned life savings, stagnant wages, government corruption, the bailout of the big banks and corporations, rising crime and societal unrest, and the virtual immunity from prosecution of some of the most blatantly corrupt elites, but what could they really do about any of these things anyway beyond complain helplessly and congregate at Tea Party rallies?

Elites expected Americans to passively accept their fate. Instead, the people did the unthinkable. They elected Donald J. Trump President of the United States.

Unlike the typical establishment politician, Trump championed the interests of American citizens, putting his life, businesses, and family at risk for the benefit of the country. As an insider, he knew the system, but chose to remain separate from it, putting God and country first. As such, he was equipped with the knowledge, tools, and character to make a real difference in the lives of ordinary citizens. Unlike the cowed media and politicians who luxuriated in the wealth of campaign contributions and freebies showered upon them by special interests, Trump was strong, resolute, and independent enough to speak truth to power and use his bully pulpit to release information the public had known and suspected all along.

The globally minded establishment predictably flew into apoplexy over his election, devoting their every effort to defeating, humiliating, and prosecuting him and removing him from office.

What could explain their reaction? Why not just wait until the next election to elect a candidate they might like better?

As will be revealed, Trump was poised to derail a nefarious secret agenda global elites had hatched for over a century earlier against the American people.

This book will divulge what those plans were and explain the method behind the madness along with a decades long agenda among elites that sought to have Communist China preside over a new world order in which the United States was to be relegated to the status of a bankrupt, third world welfare state.

Salivating over the money that stood to be made, many among the nation's corporate, political, and media elite stumbled over themselves to sell out their country and their countrymen in order to line their pockets and rise up the ranks of the new power establishment. They really thought they could not fail as long as the public remained passive, confused, and asleep. Key to their strategy was a constant barrage of fake news that was aimed as distracting and misinforming the public with a view to keeping them unsettled, powerless, and disarmed with ignorance.

The agenda of the Shadow Dragon had been quietly orchestrated behind the scenes. Hillary Clinton was to implement it as President. Giggling and dodging scandals all the way to the White House, Hillary expected to put the final nail in the proverbial American coffin and preside over America's surrender to the new world order, only something happened along the way. The American people woke up from their slumber, rebelled, and embraced nationalism with both hands. At seconds before midnight, the tide turned, and Trump was elected President, giving the country a grace period in which to save itself before the elite rose again to push through their agenda.

I wrote this book not to alarm, but to inspire discussion on this hidden agenda so that we the people of the United States and the world can fully understand what is at stake and be empowered to do something about it. I love the United States as do tens, if not hundreds of millions of other Americans.

Sadly, the United States will never recover its lost innocence, but it must retain its goodness. This harrowing chapter in American history has made us wiser and with that wisdom, we can become more thoughtful and assertive in defending our own interests within the world. We must stop allowing elites to pit the American people against other and tear our cherished country apart. No amount of money, fame, or earthly power should ever entice any of us to betray the country or the people that we love. We must defend and protect our country and its values against those who wish us harm.

Millions of noble men and women have lost their lives defending our freedoms. Once the American dream has been extinguished, the flame will never ignite again. I have faith in the American people, their goodness, spirit, and determination to restore the country, though this victory will not happen overnight. With all the power, money, and influence in the world, the traitorous elites still could not prevent a President Trump or the awakening of the American people. We still have time left to avert the fate corrupt elites have in store for us. Let us use that time wisely. This is not the time to fight among ourselves but to come together as one people under God. From there, we can forge solutions and make American great again.

Onward, patriots!

Susan Bradford

II.
The Backdoor of Socialism

The United States was founded by colonists who had fled the tyranny of Europe and its feudal class system. While the aristocrats of the old world sought to preserve their privilege, the Americans wished to preserve their freedoms and civil liberties. The colonists carefully constructed institutions that checked abuses of power. Fundamental to their belief system was the right to keep the fruits of their labor, drawing from the teachings of John Locke who affirmed private property rights. They were also guided by the Biblical parable of the talents, that God would reward those who cultivated their innate talents in service of their Creator and others.

Just as salvation was left unto the individual to accept or reject God and assume the consequences for his or her own moral decisions, enshrined within the fabric of American society was the notion of free will. The Christian faith inspired its followers to give unto the less fortunate and to engage others with integrity and compassion as their conscience guided. A moral people did not need a tyrannical government to keep them in check as they could effectively self-regulate. Their good will inspired them to love and give unto others as God had loved and given unto them. All people were equal in the eyes of the Creator.

Influenced by Christianity, Locke argued that the legitimacy of government depends upon the will of the people. Once the government loses its legitimacy, the people have a right to overthrow and replace it. Locke believed that the people were endowed by their Creator with certain inalienable rights, the right to life, liberty, and property. Since the government exists at the pleasure of the people, it is in the interests of ruling class to conduct itself fairly and justly lest it lose favor.

The free market grew from the Christian notion of fair play and competition, that one should work prudently and industriously to cultivate one's God-given talents for the glory of God, with competition bringing out the best among competitors. Rigging the system to win seemed unfair and dishonest, on par with cheating, and invited negative consequences. If the *Bible* served as their basis upon which to embrace the truth, deception was anathema to the American spirit. Seek first the kingdom of God – that is, live within God's moral prescriptions – and all the rest shall be added unto you – that is, abundance. Prosperity would follow a life lived well and righteously. From its inception, America's orientation towards the world was spiritual, as opposed to material, unlike the communists. As a result they were able to build a society consistent with God's laws. Should travesty strike, the Christian community was there to assist its fellows.

    While the American people busied themselves with their own lives, they remained oblivious to the dragon skulking in the shadows. Slinking around and through the nation's federally recognized Indian tribes were parasitic elites who harbored aspirations for world domination. The elites wished to reinforce outdated privileges drawn from the rigid European class system. The freedom loving, independently minded Americans posed a threat to the old world order. While the Americans were skeptical of any infringements upon their rights and wise to the wiles of the European aristocrats, the Indians trusted the strangers who came bearing gifts, whose words were sweeter than honey, whose greed was subtle, but insatiable, and whose inhumanity towards others was nothing short of bone chilling.

    The betrayal of the American Indians, which would later be blamed on Western values and "white man," would eventually be experienced by the American population at large. Led by the powerful, ubiquitous Rothschild banking family and its agents, the elites diligently shored up the nation's wealth, natural resources, and power within their own hands gradually and imperceptibly through the American Indian tribes.

    The truth was hidden in plain sight. After ascending to the ranks of European nobility in 1817, Nathan Rothschild adopted as the family crest the symbol of five arrows. The family crest symbolized the secret designs nursed by the Rothschilds to reclaim the lost American colony for the British crown. The Native-inspired image was designed by Moritz Oppenheim, whom the Rothschilds had commissioned for their his oil paintings. Oppenheim recounted the story of the Plutarch of Scilurus, who told his sons on his deathbed that the family would only endure if they stood together. Just as individual darts can easily be broken, bundled together they were unbreakable. So too would the Rothschilds and their allies need to stand together in order to be invincible, accounting for Hillary Clinton's "stronger together" slogan during her 2016 presidential campaign in which she used divisive rhetoric to tear the country apart carrying out the

Rothschild's communist agenda.

    The Rothschild family found strength in unity and embraced the symbol of five arrows. Each arrow represented one of Nathan's sons who would carry on the family dynasty as banker and adviser to the governments, secretly cultivating influential people throughout the world, who would derive strength in numbers through unbreakable familial bonds and friendly alliances.

    The Rothschilds gradually insinuated themselves into American institutions. Through the American Revolution, the young country secured its independence from the British Crown, which sought to expand its empire throughout the world and onto the North American continent. As the British battled the French Emperor Napoleon Bonaparte in Europe, France sold a large tract of land west of the Mississippi River for $15 million to generate money to finance its war efforts. After the French and Americans brokered the land deal through the Louisiana Purchase in 1803, the British enlisted the support of American Indians to resist expansion into the land and sought to restrict its trade, spurring the War of 1812. Though the Americans seemingly prevailed, the federal government had acquired substantial debt which the Rothschilds financed, making the country beholden to the British and its bankers once again.

    After the war, British agents influence upon the federal government to force the Indian tribes to cede their land to the U.S. government in exchange for having the federal government subsidize healthcare, education, and housing for the Indians in perpetuity. That the government made this concession is curious as the indigenous people were in no position to demand anything nor did they understand or possess a legal concept of land ownership. That this concession was made reflects that the real victor of the war was the Crown and its agents who divine a strategy which would enable them to conquer the United States through the Indian tribes.

    Growing the federal debt made the federal government beholden to the bankers."Give me control of a nation's money, and I care not who makes its laws," the Rothschilds were fond of saying. As the Rothschilds understood, the best way to conquer a people was to keep them in debt – and dependent, enabling the suppliers of goods and services to derive profits from captive, government-subsidized markets and taxpayer-supported benefits and contracts. The more indebted the federal government and people became, the more influence and control the bankers were able to wield over them. As money began to seep into the government, public servants were compromised, gradually realigning their loyalty from the people to powerful private interests.

Indians were among the first welfare recipients in the United States. Entitlements kept the Indians dependent and malleable while the tribal leaders and their supporters among the banker and corporate classes became rich through the government money they were able to obtain through the tribes for taxpayer supported products and services. Elites stoked racial tensions among Indians by blaming the rapacious looting of their resources on "white man," or the Americans. In truth, the white Christians, who had immigrated to the North American continent from Europe, sent their missionaries to the tribes in an effort to improve the lives of Indians by sharing the Gospel, helping them acquire life skills, and building schools that would empower them with education. They wanted the Indians to become independent, self-sufficient people. In contrast, the representatives of the British Crown, which fostered dependency among the Natives, endeavored to eradicate the Indian people by giving them blankets infested with smallpox. "The virus causes a disease that can inflict disfiguring scars, blindness, and death," the History Channel reported. "The tactic constitutes a crude form of biological warfare."[iii]

Since its founding, the British Crown, through its agents, has sought to subjugate the rebellious American people and reclaim the country as a vassal state for the British Empire. Rothschild tried to establish control over the country's finances by convincing Treasury Secretary Alexander Hamilton to establish the First Bank of the United States. Congress' refusal to renew the bank's charter in 1811 sent Rothschild into a fit of rage, leading him to demand that the United States return to its "colonial status." The Americans refused, resulting in the War of 1812 in which the British attempted to restrict U.S. trade and curtail America's westward expansion. The money the United States expended defending itself resulted in debt that Rothschild financed, leading to the creation of the Second Bank of the United States, which was controlled and financed by private bankers.

The robber barons and monopolists preferred the anti-competitive methods of the old world, where one's life path was determined at birth, to the freedom and competitive spirit of Americans. Given the rigidity of the European class system, the well born could expect to assume an elite position gracefully and without expending much effort while the impecunious were relegated to a life of misery and poverty, with no opportunities to rise above their station no matter how hard they tried. Competition was looked down upon by European elites whose status was conferred upon them at birth. Hard work was the labor of slaves, those of a delusional peasant class who falsely believed they could rise above their station with a little industriousness. They had to toil to support themselves lest they starve. While Americans judged the European aristocrats as effete wastrels, the Europeans looked down upon the hard working, spirited Americans as vulgarians. Reflecting the European aristocratic view, Standard Oil founder John D. Rockefeller announced that "competition is a sin." He and the other aspiring monopolists felt threatened by the energetic, resourceful upstarts in America who were keen and shameless about their desire to prove themselves and forge their own destinies in the new world.

    The monopolists sought to reinforce their privileged position by controlling as many variables as possible within the markets they coveted, with the federal government they controlled through money and other covert means, rigging the system to their advantage so that they would come out ahead no matter what.

    JP Morgan, the banker to America's burgeoning industrial elite, began his career in London. In 1895, Morgan teamed up with the Rothschilds to bail out the federal government and ease the panic of 1907. While cornering the oil market in the United States, Rockefeller relied upon the financial advice of Jacob Schiff, who presided over the Rothschild-affiliated investment bank, Kuhn, Loeb & Co. Around this time, Rockefeller, Morgan, and steel magnate Andrew Carnegie, all of whom would derive fortunes through the nation's Indian tribes, announced "our plan" to take over American industry and eliminate competition. To this end, they worked with the federal government to forge national policy "conducted by private businessmen for private gain." They also established interlocking directorships among American corporations, making them a formidable force on the national business scene. Together they were able to eliminate competition from their markets and drive rivals to financial ruin while acquiring the assets of the vanquished for pennies on the dollar.

    The illicit strategies of the robber barons proved immensely successful. By 1890, Standard Oil had cornered 88 percent of the refined oil market in the United States, making Rockefeller the first billionaire in the United States. Through manufactured crises, Wall Street tightened its grip over the nation's money supply, leading Congress to hold hearings on the concentration of power on Wall Street. Standard Oil was probed by the federal government which forced the company to break up into its component parts after it was found to have violated the Sherman Anti-Trust Act. Shortly thereafter, Rockefeller emerged as a dominant shareholder in each new company. As the years wore on, the bankers continued to tighten their control over the nation's money supply through the Federal Reserve, a private bank that served private interests.

      The monopolists often cloaked their self interest in noble rhetoric that were designed to deceive and engender support among the trusting public who were naive to the ways of the old world. With private bankers consolidating control over the nation's banks, Rockefeller and his allies sought to seize control of the nation's natural resources through the Indian tribes. Rockefeller commissioned geologists to determine which areas of land contained valuable oil and natural resources. He then dispatched Baptist missionaries to the Indian tribes to corral the Natives onto land where he and his allies were "quietly planning investments."[iv] Once the Indians settled on their new land, elite-backed attorneys descended upon Indian Country to convince the Natives to form federally recognized tribes with the promise that they could expect to govern their own sovereign nations while the federal government provided for their care. Once the tribes were federally recognized, the elites worked out how they could profit from them.

      The elites needed an air of legitimacy for their claims for public money, and so they tapped the Brookings Institution to explore the fundamental grievances in Indian Country. With Rockefeller's inner circle and the Carnegie Institute's President serving on the organization's Board of Directors, the ensuing Brookings report concluded that the fundamental grievance among Native Americans was the loss of their land.[v] In order to address this grievance, the report recommended that the federal government curtail leasing of land claimed by Indians to white settlers and use public funds to help Natives obtain loans to "buy back the lands and administer their own resources." In the process, the elites were able to claim more land on the North American continent through the tribes they controlled.

After receiving a $1,000 bribe from Nelson Rockefeller,[vi] Indian Commissioner John Collier invited Indian tribes to become federally recognized so that they could manage tribal assets and the tax-shielded businesses that were to be established on Indian reservations. The Natives were promised that they could practice their indigenous customs and that their heritage would be preserved. At the same time, they would receive generous entitlements from the federal government with Collier writing in his diary that European social democracy was to be introduced to the United States through the Indian tribes.[vii]

Once tribes became federally recognized, attorneys affiliated with the elites encouraged them to sue the federal government for compensation over the land their ancestors had lost to the federal government. The federal government then established the Indian Claims Commission, which paid out millions of dollars to the tribes as compensation. While some of the money was disbursed to the Indians, much of it was shoved out the door to private interests or shored up within tribal governments, who were used as seed capital for casinos after Sen. John McCain and his allies sponsored the Indian Gaming Regulatory Act to regulate them. The casinos were sold to the American people as a means to wean the Indians off federal money and promote tribal self-determination. Instead, the money was largely used to capitalize private businesses, with the tribal members and governments respectively receiving per capita payments and operational funding.

The wealthier tribes became, the more money they were able to pour into universities, state, local, and national political campaigns – thereby extending the reach of the elites. The elites turned around and donated generously to campaign contributions and influenced legislators to pass law ensuring that tribes would not have to account for how they managed their money or the natural resources on their land, thereby ensuring elites could seize tribal assets for themselves without having to account for what they did with it.

Tribal members were powerless to challenge the rampant corruption unfolding on their reservations. Observers could not help but notice that "elected leaders of Tribal Councils (were) middlemen for oil and uranium companies."[viii] It was not surprising, therefore, that the Navajo tribe awarded the largest concessions to Exxon (Standard Oil of New Jersey), Mobil (Standard Oil of New York), and United

Nuclear, a company co-founded by Laurance Rockefeller.

From the outset, federally recognized Indian tribes displayed an impressive level of sophistication. One hundred tribal leaders convened in 1944 to establish the National Congress of American Indians to coordinate economic development in Indian Country. The federal government was encouraged to invest in tribal businesses to help Indians become self-sufficient so that they would no longer need to rely upon federal money. Yet not only did the tribal members remain poor while wealthy tribal leaders, who served as intermediaries between the federal government and elite-controlled businesses, squandered tribal assets, but the wealthier tribes became, the more aggressively and effectively they were able to lobby the federal government for more federal dollars, as the Jack Abramoff scandal revealed.

Federally recognized Indian tribes became a cash cow for a self-perpetuating elite who conceived of an endless number of schemes to enrich themselves through government contracts and giveaways. The elites understood that if they could grow tribal populations, they could increase the number of "consumers" or their federally funded products and services. The larger the tribal populations, the wealthier they would become. Tribal Council actively recruited poor people onto tribal membership rolls, regardless of Native heritage, to increase the federal government's financial obligations to the tribes.[ix] At their inception, an Indian would need to demonstrate through genealogical records, a blood quantum of at least 1/4 Indian. As the decades wore on, that requirement was diluted until the federal government determined that for the purposes of receiving government benefits reserved for Indians, one need only be a member of a federally recognized Indian tribe.

The entitlement programs were based upon European social democratic principles conceived by Oxford-educated Baron William Beveridge, a British social reformer. The author of the *Beveridge Report* provided the intellectual foundation for the post-World War II welfare state that the British Labour government instituted in 1945. His argument that the federal government should provide a minimum standard of living "below which no one should be allowed to fall" was designed to boost the competitiveness of British industry by shifting the burden of employee benefits onto the taxpayers.

In 1964, President Lyndon B. Johnson wage a "War on

Poverty," establishing an Office of Economic Opportunity to dole out entitlements on Indian reservations. To this end, federally funded legal offices were established near Indian tribes. These offices offered free legal advice to the poor. Among the strategies recommended were acquiring tribal membership so they could receive benefits reserved for Indians. Natives watched in dismay as their sovereign nations became flooded with non-Indian outsiders who claimed voting rights and elected leaders who served elite interests over those of the indigenous Native populations. Indians complained that newcomers mocked Native customers and identities, demoralizing them further.

As the Indian Claims Commission prepared to dole out lucrative settlements to Indian tribes to compensate their members for the loss of their land, the Native American Rights Fund was established in 1971 with financial support from the Ford Foundation, the Carnegie Foundation, and the Rockefeller Foundation. NARF-affiliated attorneys worked with Tribal Councils to rewrite tribal constitutions to accommodate non-Native tribal members and the federally funded, tax-advantaged businesses, like casinos, that were being established on Indian reservations.

Richard Nixon, who succeeded LBJ as President, attempted to rein in the profligate spending of the OEO. He assigned a young congressman from Illinois by the name of Donald Rumsfeld to the task. "The OEO grew during the Johnson Administration, and so did its opposition," Rumsfeld wrote in his memoirs.[x] "When Nixon took office, it was clear that Johnson's lofty goal of eradicating poverty was failing. Hundreds of millions of dollars were being spent, and it proved difficult to identify and track progress. There was an air of radicalism in some of the OEO programs. When I first walked through the OEO offices, I saw posters of the Marxist, Che Gueverra, proudly displayed. In some parts of the country, taxpayer dollars were going to radical and violent Black Power groups. An additional controversy was that the OEO provided funds to community groups, intentionally bypassing the locally elected governors and mayors. This led to resentment of the OEO by state and local officials. Though Nixon ran on a platform hostile to the OEO, he decided after his election that he would not abolish it, but instead would try to reform it.... Nixon thought the OEO might somehow be redirected into more realistic and effective activities."

Those realistic and effective activities included helping defense contractors acquire non-compete, lucrative contracts through federally recognized Indian tribes. Despite the billions of dollars invested in these schemes, the Natives remained poor while the government contractors made out like bandits. In turn, the nation's debt continued to grow. Rumsfeld enlisted Booz Allen Hamilton, a management consulting firm, to help him develop "experimental programs" for the tribes. Among Booz's well connected clients were Canadian & Pacific Railroad and Goodyear Tire and Rubber Company. "During my tenure as Director of the OEO, we were successful in saving and strengthening some worthwhile programs by reallocating funds to them from less successful projects," Rumsfeld wrote.[xi] "We spun off functioning programs to other federal programs. We didn't perform miracles, though I believe we did some good for the poor and for the country."

During the Nixon Administration, a large pool of oil was discovered in Alaska, one that held the potential to make the United States energy independent. The elites salivated over the prospect of tapping those oil fields. Before the oil could be accessed, the federal government needed to resolve the issue of ownership over 360 million acres of land. To this end, Rumsfeld directed the OEO to finance the Alaska Federation of Natives, which led negotiations on behalf of the Natives for the land claims. The matter was resolved through the Alaska Native Claims Settlement Act, which Nixon signed into law. As part of the settlement, a billion dollars in public funds were released to the "Indians" in exchange for their land, just as they had been in the lower 48 states.

By some accounts, at least 80 percent of that money disappeared into private hands. The rest was used as seed money to develop Alaska Native Corporations. Eskimos were to be shareholders in the new businesses which were promoted as a means to help them achieve a degree of economic self-sufficiency. Predictably, ANCs quickly transformed into front groups for defense contractors, allowing elites to receive a deluge of non-compete government contracts of unlimited monetary amounts, making it easier and more profitable for them to fight their wars. Despite the profitability these businesses would enjoy in the decades ahead, the Eskimos remained poor, enabling elites to petition the federal government time and time again for federal funds for their care. Elites facilitated government contracts that would help lift Natives out of poverty. While the politically connected became rich through these contracts, the Eskimos languished in poverty.

The ANCs were set up as a vehicle to enrich the political classes and their corporate allies. In 1987, the Carlyle Group was established after David Rubenstein learned about a tax loophole forged by Sen. Ted Stevens that enabled ANCs to "leverage their losses by selling them to profitable companies looking for a break on their taxes," Dan Briody wrote in <u>The Iron Triangle: Inside the Secret World of the Carlyle Group.</u> "Before long, they were flying Eskimos into Washington, DC, buttering them up, and brokering deals between them and profitable American companies....(They) couldn't get enough free money....(and so) a cottage industry (was) born... (They) recognized the ongoing potential of the business and decided to incorporate....With a crew in place, liabilities limited, and money coming in the door...,they decided to ... establish a company on a scheme that denied the federal government close to $1,000,000,000 in taxes....Everyone's happy but the taxpayers." The ANCs, the *Washington Monthly* reported, created "endless subsidiaries so that the parent firms could have indefinite access to contracts."[xii]

Within Carlyle, a nexus of powerful, politically connected liberals and neoconservatives intertwined like a double helix. "Carlyle would never have gotten to the level that it is at today had it not been for this premeditated commingling of business and politics," Briody wrote.[xiii] The firm aggressively recruited former high ranking government officials while investing in companies and interests regulated by the former agencies that employed them. George Soros, a billionaire financier who has endowed the Native American Rights Fund and the National Congress of American Indians, invested $100,000,000 in Carlyle Partners II, one of the largest and most successful Carlyle funds. The firm also employed George W. Bush before he became governor. The governor turned around and invested $10,000,000 in the firm. Rumsfeld went on to serve as Chairman while his former OEO assistant, Dick Cheney, presided over Halliburton, an oil company that acquired federal contracts through ANCs during the War on Iraq when Bush was President and Rumsfeld was Secretary of Defense. Former President George H.W. Bush got in on the game too, serving as adviser to Carlyle while his son was President.

Carlyle now manages accounts valued at over $157,000,000,000, making it the ninth largest Pentagon contractor between 1998 and 2003. By 2011, David Rubenstein, who founded the firm, boasted a net worth of $2,800,000,000, earning him the rank of the 138th richest person in the United States. His wife, Alice Rogoff Rubenstein, who had worked for *Washington Post* publisher Donald Graham and served as CFO for the *U.S. News and World Report*, became publisher of the *AlaskaDispatch.com*, an influential online news magazine which shapes political discourse in Alaska. "(Alice) now wields even more political influence over Alaskan, American and global politics," the *Anchorage Press* reported. "She has enough power and money to win over candidates from pretty much every persuasion."[xiv]

Between 1997 and 2005, ANCs received a reported $4,400,000,000 in contracts. The Wars on Iraq and Afghanistan, which had depleted the national treasury of $2,400,000,000,000 by 2017, spurred a bonanza of taxpayer-supported contracts for the ANCs. One ANC subsidiary, Nana Pacific, for example, received a $70,000,000 contract with the Department of Defense to rebuild an Iraqi port. Over $225,000,000 in military construction contracts were awarded to Olgoonik Corporation, a Native village corporation based in a small village of Wainwright, Alaska, which assigned the work to Halliburton. The Chugach Alaska Corporation generated revenues of $700,000,000 for work ranging from monitoring seismic activity from a base in Korea to running military bases – and another $2,500,000,000 operating the Ronald Reagan Ballistic Missile Defense Test Site.[xv] Among the defense contractors that contracted through the ANCs were Bechtel and Lockheed Martin.

Lance Morgan, the President of Ho-Chunk Native Corporations and Chairman of the Native American Contractors Association told the Senate Indian Affairs Committee: "Our government systems were imposed upon us. You could not have designed a worse economic system – bad legal, bad government, no control of our assets, and socialism...Now I run this corporation that started as one employee....I made myself CEO. We have 1,400 employees now in five different countries. You would have to come to rural Nebraska to even believe how strange that is..... In the first year, we had revenues of $400,000, and I remember thinking, 'We had $12,000 this week, and that is pretty good'. Well, we did $193,000,000 last year....What is interesting, when I brought up the idea of starting a corporation, everyone basically was against the idea because we had failed at every business we had ever tried (until we) got into government contracting...If you were to take these things away, we would fall right back into poverty. How are maintaining these programs helping Natives achieve self-sufficiency? The fact is, they aren't. If we were to go backwards, we would go back on food stamps. We would cost the government a fortune. Taking thousands of people off government assistance and giving them hope is the way to go."

Despite being the greatest recipients of federal funds, tribal members remain among the poorest in the nation. "Reservation poverty is so pronounced, it can be clearly seen on national maps, with hot spots of poverty in the northern plains, eastern Arizona, southeastern Utah, and western New Mexico, which overlap directly with Indian reservations," a spokesman for the National Congress of American Indians said. "The billions spent in Indian Country have hardly made a dent in the well being of Indians." The solution proposed was always to spend billions more.

Where was all the money going? Following the money is difficult as the federal government ensured that tribal organizations do not have to account for how their money is spent. They could hide behind the impenetrable walls of tribal sovereignty and ignore FOIA requests. What is clear is that the intended beneficiaries were not the Indians. As Alaska Sen. Dennis DeConcini told the Senate Indian Affairs Committee in 1989, "A majority of companies who represented themselves as legitimate Indian contractors are, in fact, secretly backed or controlled by nonIndian firms. These so-called Indian companies that include the largest construction firms active on Indian lands, receive Indian preference from the Department of Housing and Urban Development, the Bureau of Indian Affairs, and the Small Business Administration, which were approved by the Bureau of Indian Affairs as legitimate contractors."

Around the time that a deluge of wealth began to flow into Indian Country, the leading investment firms of the elites, Goldman Sachs and Morgan Stanley simultaneously decided to go public with an IPO in 1986. As the elite banks and industrialists must have appreciated, tribal casinos and Alaska Native Corporations stood to generate hundreds of millions to billions of dollars per year a piece, providing easy access to virtually unlimited amounts of capital.

Once a decision was made to go public, virtually overnight Goldman Sachs "transformed into a trading powerhouse, one that would challenge top ranking Salomon Brothers, which was operating with considerably more capital," Lisa Endlich wrote in <u>Goldman Sachs: the Culture of Success</u>. At the same time, Goldman Sachs "decided that it wanted to be a great global firm....The instinct of the organization were that, without knowing how we could get that capital, there was a leap of faith, that we could achieve our goals. I think it was instinctive, not a studied decision. In 1986, the plans for international expansion were mostly just talk. The firm had a few foreign offices, one each in Switzerland, Tokyo, London, and Hong Kong .... The goal of the firm was to build the premier investment banking firm that would dominate every aspect of business. It would be an astonishing feat, one that no firm had achieved before. In 1986, there were many investment banks in contention for the top spot, and the outcome of the race was far from assured."

While Goldman Sachs was reaching for the brass ring, Morgan Stanley, whose client roster includes six of the seven sister oil companies, and General Motors, also decided to go public. Morgan Stanley was booking over $82 million in net income, up to $1 million from the first quarter of 1989 while "some firms were reporting gigantic losses," Patricia Beard wrote in <u>Blue Blood & Mutiny</u>. The firm, she wrote, was described as "the most profitable" on Wall Street, with earnings in 1990 of $443 million on $2.5 billion in revenue. "Prior to 1986, Morgan Stanley partners could expect to become 'respectably rich in a respectable way,'...but not hugely -- even excessively -- rich....As the risk-reward equation was heightened, Wall Street attracted people who were less interested in first class business than in the promise of mega-paydays."

The injection of capital evidently came from Japan's Sumitomo Bank, which hired a top consulting firm, McKinsey and Co., to advise its executives on the best way to enter the American market. A founding corporate member of the Council on Foreign Relations, McKinsey suggested Goldman Sachs. Never before had the bank taken outside equity. However, by offering to make a $500 million investment in exchange for 12.5 percent of the firm's profits, Sumitomo had valued Goldman Sachs at $4 billion -- or more than four times its book value. During Morgan Stanley and Goldman Sach's initial public offering, GM and Ford retained McKinsey to advise them on their own corporate restructuring. The Sumitomo deal, Endlich wrote, "would be conducted in total secrecy, with Goldman Sachs acting as its own investment banker. "

Within a few years, as taxpayer-subsidized tribal casinos and ANCs churned out records amounts of money; a deluge of capital poured into Goldman Sachs and Morgan Stanley vis-à-vis Sumitomo Bank in Japan, providing equity for their respective Mergers & Acquisitions divisions; as a result, these firms were able to help their elite clients dramatically outpace the competition and balloon into entities that would become "too big to fail," further consolidating money, power, and control on Wall Street.[xvii]

Goldman Sachs' capitalization, a modest $200 million in 1990 had grown to $1 billion in only six years. During this period, the firm's return on equity reached as high as 80 percent, far outstripping the industry norm.

In 1995, Merrill Lynch, the largest U.S investment bank, had only managed a return of equity of 10 percent while the more competitive Morgan Stanley earned 34 percent.

As a result of this capitalization, by 1994, Goldman Sachs was able to negotiate some of the biggest financial deals in history, including the $13 billion privatization of Deutsche Telekom, the $38 billion merger of Daimler-Benz and Chrysler Corporation, and the first privatization of China Telecom. Goldman Sachs owned the largest block of stock ever transacted -- 17 million shares of British Petroleum, or roughly the amount of shares in the oil company that traded in a normal month.

In 1994, Endlich recalled, "a Goldman Sachs' partner of considerable seniority gushed that he had met with a member of the Federal Reserve Board who had informed him that 'We're too big to fail. A $100 million loss, a $50 million loss, it means nothing. We're too big now. They won't let us fail'."

***

Elites had long appreciated that great profits stood to be generated through federally funded infrastructure projects, entitlement programs, and corporate welfare. The Bush dynasty is the poster family of corporate welfare. Consider, for example, that while his father was President of the United States, George W. Bush was awarded $200,000,000 in public funds to build a sports stadium for the Texas Rangers. While George H.W. Bush was Vice President, his other son, Neil Bush, became caught up in the Savings and Loans scandals of the 1980s as a member of the Board of Directors of Silverado Savings and Loan in which the young Bush became ensnared over alleged "breaches of fiduciary duties involving multiple conflicts of interest."[xvii]

Nelson Rockefeller, the grandson of the Standard Oil founder, financed 88,000 low income housing units through "moral obligation" bonds subsidized by taxpayers. A substantial portion of the state's subsidized housing was financed through Rockefeller's New York Urban Development Corporation before he received public money to develop the Love Canal, Roosevelt Island, and Niagara Falls. After pocketing a small fortune, the NYDC filed for bankruptcy.

President Barack Obama's advisor Valerie Jarrett amassed a fortune through subsidized public housing as did Fox News host Sean Hannity who reportedly leveraged his political connections to secure HUD mortgages to purchase valuable real estate after the banks foreclosed on the previous owners.

The disastrous policies that were wrecking havoc on the U.S. economy had been discreetly nurtured in Indian Country as evidenced by the S&L debacle.

In the 1980s, the Reagan Administration, which was ostensibly fighting communism throughout the world, weakened the power of the Federal Home Loan Bank Board to regulate Savings and Loans on grounds that limiting governmental regulation would help the economy flourish. This might have been a prudent policy had Wall Street and the banks been run by honorable people working within parameters that enforced prudent policy, prosecuted and penalized bad actors, and limited the damage of reckless actors. Instead, the government cleared the way for elites to invest the people's money in speculative ventures that allowed them to profit on a good day and leave the public holding the bag on a bad one.

Properly incentivized, S&Ls acquired valuable real estate by limiting the amount of capital reserves thrifts were required to hold to cover loans; in turn, they were able to secure low interest loans with high interest dividends.

Eager to take advantage of these opportunities, the First Navajo Savings and Loans Association League tapped Navajo Chief Peter MacDonald to establish a new S&L branch office in Window Rock, Arizona.[xviii] MacDonald, who presided over billions of dollars worth of uranium and coal deposits on Navajo land, was well schooled in the elite ethos. He had also served on Nixon's Committee to Re-elect the President. As Chief, MacDonald used the S&L to secure a loan for an industrial park to help the Southern Union Gas Company and Mountain Bell "extend a gas line ... to the (Bureau of Indian Affairs) Boarding School" and offer services "required by large industrial firms."

The muckraking publication *Mother Jones*[xix] attributed his rise to "Anglo acculturation" which began "the moment he set foot in a (Bureau of Indian Affairs) school." As a result of this acculturation, *Mother Jones* reported, "MacDonald achieved nearly unbreakable control over the Navajo's destiny, dispensing patronage and punishment at will. He has set the reservation's economy on a course that many economists, environmentalists, and anthropologists predict will destroy Navajo and their livelihood by the end of the century."

While the Navajo reservation was exporting enough energy reserves "to meet the needs of the whole state of Arizona for 32 years," *Mother Jones* reported, "the Navajo people remain some of the poorest on the continent." Reminiscent of a third word communist dictator, who relied upon the cult of personality, MacDonald's portrait hung on the walls of OEO offices across the nation. "Like antipoverty administrators in so many American ghettos, MacDonald was able to parlay control of welfare into an awesome political base," *Mother Jones* reported. "He'd come into Council chambers and deliver fiery speeches against the white man, the BIA, and energy companies."

McDonald also excelled at virtual signaling. While promising to secure generous entitlements for tribal members, he succeeded principally in creating a "sprawling, voracious bureaucracy over which he had almost complete control." *Mother Jones* reported.

The Navajo reservation, bore all the hallmarks of elite control including a "classic Third World colony" appearance along with "visible signs of wealth and status in bureaucratic Window Rock surrounded by a sea or rural poverty and helplessness," *Mother Jones* reported. As Tribal Chairman, McDonald controlled "the Council, the courts, the committees, the police." Opponents of his regime were crushed, denied funds, and targeted for political attacks. Elite strategies developed within Indian Country eventually was applied to the country at large.

The most infamous of those implicated in the S&L scandals

was Charles Keating, Jr., who presided over American Continental Corporations and the Lincoln Savings and Loan Association. "Thanks to federally insured deposits, (Keating) could get almost any amount of money, and the government would guarantee the folks who loaned it to him," Michael Binstein and Charles Bowden wrote in <u>Trust Me: Charles Keating and the Missing Billions.</u> "He could do with this money pretty much anything he wanted."

While scouting for real estate, Keating, who had cultivated powerful political contacts while serving on Nixon's Commission on Obscenity and Pornography, joined Mother Teresa of Calcutta to a remote Indian reservation in the southwest.[xx] Binstein and Bowden reported that Keating sadistically taunted his employees with a "cheap poster of an American Indian Chief poster that "moved around the office" when he was about to fire them.

Keating was cognizant of the secrets of the tribes and sought to capitalize on that insider knowledge. After the Nixon Administrated intervened on behalf of the Hopi Indians in a Hopi-Navajo land dispute, Keating "stumbled upon a huge parcel about twenty miles west of Phoenix in a high desert valley tucked away in the Estrella Mountains"[xxi]

For decades, the Navajo and Hopi had been fighting over a joint use area in northern Arizona when a local rancher offered to trade his land to the Navajos for a parcel of land held by the Bureau of Land Management near Phoenix in the foothills of the Estrella Mountains. "The deal goes through, and (Keating) immediately goes to the (American Continental Corporation, which owns Lincoln Savings and Loan)," Binstein and Bowden wrote. "They are in a buying frenzy, and best of all, they pay top dollar." Keating had found "the deal of the decade, thousands of perfect acres ready for development...He will not do a subdivision. He will not do a little retirement community. He will not add one more tract to the sprawl of Phoenix...He will build a city of 200,000 people. He will bring in industry. He will create an international airport. He will create a total world, one that will ignore Phoenix. It will look West. It will advertise itself as Los Angeles' latest addition, a mere six hours or so down the freeway, a place where housing is cheaper, where labor is cheaper, where factories can be built away from all the costs of southern California." Like drunken sailors, bankers splurged on public money until the S&Ls went belly up costing taxpayers $125,000,000,000 in losses.

***

Emboldened by the ease through which they were able to siphon public funds through Indian tribes, politically connected elites devised ever more schemes to use federally recognized tribal nations to shore up the nation's wealth, resources, and land into their own hands. Among their favorite strategies was to parlay the betrayal of groups they had victimized into profitable, heart-wrenching grievances over which they could sue the federal government for millions -- and if they could get away with it, billions, of dollars to compensate the victims, and by extension, themselves, for the damage either they or their progenitors had inflicted. The famous *Cobell* class action is a case in point.

The smiling, affable Elouise Cobell was the face of the litigation that bore her name. Even though she had pursued her class action for over a decade, the defendant listed in the suit was Ken Salazar, the Secretary of Interior in the Obama Administration, who represented the Department of Interior which was assigned responsibility for over a century's worth of mismanagement of Indian land and resources that the government had held in trust for the American Indians.

The granddaughter of a legendary Indian Chief, Cobell was born on the oil-rich Blackfeet reservation in 1945. Two decades earlier, Blackfeet Chief Wolf Plume had received financial support from John D. Rockefeller and christened Rockefeller's grandson Laurance. Standard Oil established gas stations around the reservation.[xxii]

Followed a tried and true elite formula, Cobell established the Blackfeet National Bank to raise capital for infrastructure and business development projects within Indian Country. In order to meet the growing demand for capital, the bank pooled its assets with other tribes to form the Native American Bank, which listed Alaska Native Corporations, the Navajo Nation, the Mashantucket Pequot, and the Seminole Tribe of Florida as shareholders.

A recipient of a "genius award" from the MacArthur Foundation, which partners with nonprofit organizations and foundations affiliated with Rockefeller (Standard Oil), Alfred P. Sloan

(President and CEO of General Motors), Charles Stewart Mott (General Motors), Ford (Ford Motors), Carnegie, and other wealthy progressive, industrialist families, Cobell teamed up with the Indian Land Capital Company for capital to purchase lands that were separated from Indian tribes, and the companies that controlled them, through acts of legislation. Cobell also served on the Board of the Northwest Area Foundation, which sponsored an Annual Indian Land Consolidation program that "impacts federal Indian policy regarding Indian land issues."

After graduating from Great Falls Business College, Cobell was appointed tribal treasurer. In this role, Cobell stumbled upon accounting irregularities with regards to oil and gas extraction on the Blackfeet reservation. Based upon her research, Cobell concluded that tribes were owed hundreds of billions of dollars from the federal government over "white man's" theft of tribal land and natural resources.

The Native American Rights Fund joined Cobell in a class action law suit to force the federal government to reform its management of tribal trust funds, with financial support provided by the Ford Foundation and Blackfeet Reservation Development Fund. "Early on we were told the genius of the strategy of the case, that it was not asking for money, so it would not run any red flags up the polls," a tribal chairman told Congress.[xxiii] "It was simply asking for a correct accounting, a reconciliation, and that is why it was able to be brought in the federal District Court as a declaratory and injunctive matter....But in order to get monetary damages, that requires a sovereign immunity from the United States, likely a judicial referral. The settlement cannot be done solely by the Executive branch. The Administration requires (Congress') stamp of approval on it....I know that there were very warm feelings for (NARF) at that time, and that we thought (NARF) was going to win $170,000,000,000 with NARF getting its fair share of that. However, NARF was not even listed as class counsel. I'm sure they recognize at this point that there are some very sort of dangerous conflicts of interest for them putting it in there today. But I can tell you at that time that that is the discussion that we had."

Arthur Andersen, a now-defunct accounting firm that had audited Enron, determined that between 1973 and 1992, the federal government could not account for $2,400,000,000 in Indian trust money, Cobell filed her suit in 1996. Two years later, the Department of Interior failed to produce the court-ordered documents after the Treasury Department reported that at least 16 Federal Reserve banks and branches shredded key Indian trust documents relevant to the case. While receiving financial support from the Ford Foundation and Blackfeet Reservation Development Fund, Cobell and her team sloughed through more than 3,600 court filings, 220 days of trial, 80 published court decisions, and 10 appeal, making little progress.

Her luck changed with the election of President Barack Obama who agreed to have taxpayers give the plaintiffs $3,400,000,000 to settle the suit even though the evidence relevant to the case had been destroyed. JP Morgan Chase, a Rockefeller-affiliated bank, served as depositor for the plaintiffs in what became one of the biggest class action payouts to Indian tribes in history. Having been adopted as an honorary tribal member to the energy-rich Crow Nation, Obama was loyal to tribal interests, or at least to the interests that controlled the them.

The American Indian Trust Management Reform Act established the statutory basis for the *Cobell* suit, reaffirming the federal government's obligation to properly account for Indian trust funds. Once the act was signed into law, a class action was filed on behalf of over 300,000 Indian account holders.

"Since the turn of the century, the government has collected billions of dollars from farming and grazing leases, timber sales, and oil and gas production on Indian lands, money which is supposed to have been ultimately disbursed to its rightful Indian owner," a NARF spokesman declared. "Whether this occurred or not is anyone's guess, however, because never once in over one hundred years has the government bothered to account for the Indian trust funds under its control....The suit charges, among other things, that the federal government has breached its legally-mandated trust responsibility to prudently manage trust assets belonging to individual Indian trust beneficiaries and has consistently refused to fix an accounting system that it has admitted is fundamentally flawed and completely ineffective in accounting for these assets. As a result, billions of dollars belonging to individual Indians remain to this day unaccounted for." The plaintiffs stood to receive $1,500 a piece for the settlement, hardly a life changing amount of money.

After the plaintiffs exhausted their appeals in court, in 2010, the House Committee on Natural Resources agreed to hold hearings to determine the verdict. The proposed $3,400,000,000 settlement included $1,500,000,000 for claims to individual Indians. The remaining $1,900,000,000 was set aside to address a fractionated Indian lands issue, essentially allowing the federal government to buy the land back for the Indians at market value so that the tribes could pursue economic development. Of the amount sought, between $50 and $100 million were to be set aside for attorney fees.

"This decision will help make amends for past mismanagement of Indian trust funds by the U.S. Government," said Dale Kildee, a Democratic Congressman from Flint, Michigan. "While this is an important issue, this is not the end of the fight for justice on behalf of Indian trust assets, and I will continue to fight to ensure that *our tribes* are treated in a fair and equitable manner. I, along with several of my colleagues, will be sending a letter to House leadership urging them to provide immediate assistance and support in passing legislation to approve and fund the *Cobell v. Salazar* Settlement Agreement."

Secrecy surrounded the settlement as the case moved forward in Congress. Resolution could have been achieved "much sooner but for the strategy of the Obama Administration and the plaintiffs to avoid public hearings, a separate vote on the merits of the deal, and opportunities to amend it to correct significant flaws identified by respected tribal organizations and leaders, individual Indian allottees, and trust reform experts," the *Tribal Business Journal* reported.

Among the most voluble critics of *Cobell* was University of Wisconsin-Madison Law Prof. Richard Monette, who went so far as to suggest collusion among the participating parties. "In August 2009, the plaintiff's lawsuit took a steep turn for the worse," he told Congress. "In many people's eyes, to invoke the vernacular, the case had tanked. The federal District Court ruled that an accounting was not possible and ordered defendants to pay $455,000,000 in restitution.... Therefore, at best, the settlement should be limited to the $455,000,000 that the District Court ordered as restitution. At worst, the settlement should be void, and the Department should set about the task of accounting as the Court of Appeals ordered.... The *Cobell* lawsuit fell victim to collusion at the expense of the American taxpayer....But generally that has been a percentage of an amount that the Court has ordered, and here the Court ordered $455,000,000. Then we got two sides that basically colluded to add more money to that, and then for attorneys' fees to be added...."

The plundering of the nation's financial and natural resources through the tribes was just the beginning...

One outgrowths of the *Cobell* settlement was the creation of an Indian Land Consolidation Center which the federal government established to acquire as many fractionated interests as possible to consolidate these land interests so Indian tribes could pursue tribal self-determination and fulfill economic, social, and cultural development needs while reducing government administrative costs. The new program was reportedly expected to cost the Department of Interior $285,000,000 to run.

As part of the settlement, a Tribal Trust Accounting Program was created at the Department of Interior to acquire fair market value for the fractional interest in trust or restricted lands that individual Indian land owners were willing to sell back to the Department. The program was called the Land Buyback Program for Indian Nations, which focused on 40 reservations in the Great Plains and Rocky Mountain areas, most of which are energy rich members of the Council of Energy Resource Tribes, whose correspondence address is Greenberg Traurig, the firm at the center of the Abramoff scandal. Once the land was acquired, the tribe and the interests which controlled them could exploit those resources to maximum effect.

As the national deficit spiraled out of control, federal legislators voiced concern about the viability of continued payouts to tribes by way of settlement through legislation. In 2011, Congressman Doc Hastings told the *Tribal Business Journal*, "This past November, the American people sent a clear message to Congress: reduce spending, focus on job creation, and perform your constitutional duty to oversee the Executive Branch's policies and decisions. As Chairman of the Natural Resources Committee, I plan to make all three of those efforts a top priority this Congress....Regarding tribal trust lawsuits, I would be interested in ascertaining the status of the lawsuits and a careful examination of the risks and liabilities of continuing the litigation. The federal debt just reached $14,000,000,000,000 and under the deficit reduction rules being implemented in the House of Representatives, it may be difficult to resolve lawsuits by an act of Congress without a full understanding of the risks, liabilities, and costs associated with them."

***

Though Cobell never lived to see the disbursement of checks, she would savor her victory which she described as bittersweet. "I would have liked to have gotten more than $3,400,000,000," she told Congress. "I wanted $280,000,000,000 at one point in time, but what is reasonable? What is reasonable during this time before so many people pass away and die, and die of poverty. And we were asking for $48,000,000,000. The Court came back and said, no, I think I will give you $455,000,000, and then the Appellate Court said, well, go back to District Court, and said, oh, the government can do any type of an accounting that they want....It was very important to us to have people understand that this would not be taxable. Many of the people that are going to be receiving this money are poor. Entitlement programs are very important to them, and the majority of people are on SSI...on food stamps, and we wanted to ensure that those were not disrupted."

In 2011, Cobell succumbed to cancer at the age of 65. Before she died, she envisioned her legacy, telling reporters that she hoped future generations of Natives would fight for their rights just as she did. "Maybe one of these days, they won't even think about me," she said. "They'll just keep going and say, 'This is because I did it.' I never started this case with any intentions of being a hero. I just wanted this case to give justice to people that didn't have it."

While the merits of the case were debatable or perhaps the blame improperly assigned, Cobell inspired deep admiration and respect from those who knew her. "Many people have worked on the reform issue over the years, and they have moved on," Congressman Nick Rahall told the House Resources Committee. "The one constant through it all has been Elouise Cobell....She has not once faltered in her mission to mend the system and ensure that future Indian allottees benefit from a well managed trust fund process, and I would be remiss if I did not take a moment to reflect on what has brought us to this point – over 100 years of mismanagement of Indian trust funds by the United States and decades of ignoring the problem."

After her passing, Cobell's legacy lived on with tribes waging lawsuits against the federal government for mismanagement and abuses of one sort or another. Yet, President Barack Obama, whose tribal name means "one who helps all people of this land," continued to dispense "justice" to Indian Country, with four tribes in the Dakotas reaching a $100,000,000 deal with his Administration to resolve a legal dispute. Another $1,000,000,000 was released to dozens of other tribes for alleged government mismanagement of royalties for oil, gas, grazing, and timber on tribal lands. The only tribe of people whom Obama did not seem concerned with helping were the ordinary American taxpayers who were footing the bill.

In the meantime, nearly all of the 1,500,000 acres of the Blackfeet reservation have been leased for oil and gas exploration, much to the chagrin of conservationists who are trying to curb development efforts. Anschutz was among the three main oil and gas companies active on the reservation. In the 1980s, Anschutz, whose media holdings included the neoconservative *Weekly Standard*, reportedly sold a half interest in its one billion barrel oil pocket on Anschutz Ranch for $500,000,000 to Mobil Oil, a direct descendant of Standard Oil.

Yet, while the Blackfeet tribe savored this payout, the federal government turned a blind eye to the growing corruption on its reservation. In a column published in the *Missoulian* in 2013, William Old Chief, a former Blackfeet Chairman and member of the Blackfeet Tribal Business Council, spoke to the Obama Administration's indifference to tribal mismanagement.

"I was reminded of all the Blackfeet members who have written (to the President) or those in the U.S. Interior Department asking for some type of intervention concerning the lawlessness now existing on the Blackfeet reservation, but not once has he answered their request," he wrote. "This is the same man who promised Indian Country change if we would vote for him. Crime has gone rampant on the reservation because there is no leadership; as a matter of fact, it is the leadership who is breaking the law and telling law enforcement, 'You can't touch me, I'm sovereign'....Millions of taxpayer dollars are wasted, stolen, or misused, and no one cares. The (Bureau of Indian Affairs), when asked for assistance in this matter that has existed since Aug. 27, 2012, reply that it's an internal conflict. What about the trust responsibility they talk about when it comes to our money from tribal resources and now the Elouise Cobell record $3,400,000,000 settlement...? We are under Marshall Law (sic) and if the people speak up or stand up, they will be put down at any cost...The U.S. Department of Interior is not welcome to intervene in the issues of the Blackfeet people because we are a 'sovereign nation.' As long as the federal government continues to funnel millions of dollars onto the Blackfeet reservation with corrupt people ... corruption will flourish under the umbrella of sovereignty and self-determination. Washington! Stop the corruption and lawlessness on the Blackfeet Indian Reservation! Please!"

Through relationships cultivated through the Indians tribes, the European socialist elites and their corporate allies who were working with and through the federal government to enrich themselves at the expense of the American people would continued to claim public land, plunder public funds, and seize natural resources for their own private use, becoming obscenely rich and powerful in the process.

The Natives have long known the secrets of the elites, having experienced their shadowy manipulations firsthand. If the tribes provided the means through which the elites could gradually reshape the United States into the socialist mold, the first and second World Wars would draw the country into their dynastic battles, providing European elites the wherewithal to open and establish enduring lines of communication throughout the American intelligence and journalism communities; in the process, they would acquire the means to manipulate the political process and public perception through back channels while managing public discourse to avoid detection and prosecution for decades to come.

III.
Back Channels of the Deep State

  Few could have anticipated the good fortune that would befall Cornelius Vander Starr. Born in 1892 to struggling European immigrants, Vander Starr was unremarkable by any measure. He was raised on the Pomo Indian reservation in Mendocino County, California where a military post, Ft. Bragg, had been established to keep settlers at bay while elites extracted the resources. Resident lumber mills processed trees and shipped the wood to local ports and rail lines. His father worked as an engineer on the California Western Railroads alongside Chinese coolies.

  Against all odds, Starr rose from obscurity to preside over one of the largest, most profitable insurance companies in the world. He was an overnight sensation. "Some men leave an indelible mark on their colleagues without planning to do so," the Starr Foundation reminisced. "Yet, so content are they on living and working and doing that they find neither the time nor the patience for keeping any records of what they have accomplished or how they lived. Starr was such a man whose brilliance and remarkable energy were matched only by a passion for anonymity that amounted to almost shyness. But where the mark of a man has been left, it can be found."

  Before his career took flight, Starr's mother opened the family house to boarders while the young Starr swept the halls of the local branch of the Odd Fellows, an international fraternity founded in England in 1066. Odd Fellows recruited men from the trades and lower classes to help them establish businesses, provide for their welfare, and collaborate with each other to dominate local markets, propelling many to success that would not have realized on their own.[xxiv] They were, as Rothschild would have it, stronger together. President Franklin D. Roosevelt, and a number of senators, governors, and presidents were counted among its members.

  As a young man, the ambitious Starr enrolled in UC Berkeley, the most prestigious of the universities within the UC system, only to drop out soon after to work for a realty company where he specialized in insurance. Reminiscent of today's celebrity children, Starr passed the California state bar exam without having attended law school or graduated from college.

  With influential figures supporting him, Starr enlisted in the

U.S. Army, but never deployed. Instead he was assigned to work for the Pacific Mail Steamship, a New York joint stock company that established mail routes and back channels through San Francisco, Hong Kong, Yokohama, and Shanghai. Henry Morton, the Steamship's captain, managed several hotels in Shanghai, including the famous Astor House, the Chinese affiliate of the eponymous luxury hotel established in New York City by John Jacob Astor who had made his fortune selling opium, the drug that financed the British Empire. Starr would soon be headed to Shanghai.

The Pacific Mail Steamship was the property of William Averell Harriman, the son of a railroad baron who attended Groton School and Yale University. Harriman served on the National Recovery Administration, which restrained competition to elite businesses. He also coordinated the Lend-Lease program which armed the British against the Nazis while Brown Brothers & Harriman provided assistance to the industrialists who backed the Nazi regime, reflecting strategies employed by elites to profit by supporting both sides of a war. After the Second World War, Harriman coordinated the Marshall Plan which left taxpayers on the hook for $12,000,000,000 to rebuild a postwar Europe . As a result, corporate giants that had profited from war were able to profit again through the reconstruction effort.

With powerful contacts in hand, Starr relocated to China, where extra-territoriality granted him special rights reserved for foreigners to establish s business in China under the law of their home country. During the Second World War, Starr quickly rose to prominence by assisting the Allies through back channel communications and intelligence sharing. In his new home, Starr was inspired by the vast untapped markets of China which promised to make him exceeding rich through insurance sales. "The providential and family loving Chinese would naturally be attracted to the principle of life insurance, though which they could pass on the fulfillment of their own hopes to their families," the Starr Foundation affirmed.

After Starr established American Asiatic Underwriters, Inc., he insured risks for high value clients, including a baseball team and Jewish refugees fleeing from Vladivostok, Russia to mainland Europe on a Czech ship.

Starr became an overnight sensation.

At 27 years of age, he had managed to create the largest

insurance company in the world. With money bursting from his pockets, he acquired the *Shanghai Evening Post,* which reported news of interest to the Shanghai business community. As publisher, he cultivated Henry Luce, the China-born publisher of *Fortune*, *Sports Illustrated,* and *Time* magazine, and recruited such luminaries as Randall Gould, a correspondent for *Time, United Press International,* and the *Christian Science Monitor;* and John Ahlers, a correspondent for the *Economist*, an international news magazine owned by the Rothschild-backed Economist Group. Starr published his newspapers a few blocks away from his insurance headquarters so that his Shanghai offices could communicate with each other through chit coolie. As Starr discovered, insurance underwriting granted him access to sources and information that otherwise would have eluded him and his news gathering operation.

As the World Wars raged through Europe, President Franklin D. Roosevelt set up an informal intelligence apparatus called the Office of Strategic Services, through which elites passed along vital information drawn from their international networks. Starr was encouraged to insure the property of the U.S. Service men, the Germans, Nazis, and Japanese as part of OSS intelligence gathering efforts. Journalists and insurance agents were perceived as valuable intelligence assets for the war effort given their ability to penetrate difficult to reach places, cultivate sources, and acquire vital information outsiders would not have been privy to. "Newspapers everywhere are expected to stick their noses in everybody's business (and provide) almost indestructible cover for the collection of information." a former OSS officer told reporters.

Thanks to the OSS, the Allies could identify "which factories to burn, which bridges to blow up, (and) which cargo ships could be sunk in good conscience," *The Los Angeles Times* reported. "They ultimately brought down Adolf Hitler's Third Reich." The Insurance Intelligence Unit, a component of the Office of Strategic Services and its elite counterintelligence branch, gathered intelligence on the enemy's insurance industry, blueprints for bomb plants, timetables of tide changes, among others details about Nazi targets. Led by Starr, the OSS insurance unit enabled the Allies to cripple Hitler's industrial base and undermine the morale of the German people by incinerating their cities.

Prior to the creation of the OSS, the executive branch had

conducted American intelligence gathering loosely and on an *ad hoc* basis Once the United States was drawn into the Second World War, British intelligence convinced the U.S. federal government to recruit a Republican lawyer by the name of William "Wild Bill" Donovan to establish an informal intelligence gathering service based upon the British Secret Intelligence Service (M16) and Special Operations Executive.

By accommodating Britain, "America (was propelled) permanently onto the world stage," former CIA Director Stanfield Turner said.[xxv] "Roosevelt did not know at the time that he had just paved the way for Donovan to enter his inner circle of advisers and that doing so would lead to the creation of America's first fully fledged intelligence service."

A lieutenant colonel who invested with the Rockefeller-controlled National City Bank, Donovan would eventually become one of the most decorated men in U.S. history. The OSS recruited individuals from elite families, many of whom owed their allegiance and affluence to their service and ties to the British Crown and its affiliated corporate allies. Among its recruits was Vincent Astor of the prominent Astor family, who made a fortune smuggling opium, the drug that financed the British Empire. Astor acquired *Newsweek* and gathered intelligence through a secret society called The Room in which elites were plied with alcohol, the original truth serum, and invited to divulge their most closely guarded secrets. One of his adventures involved joining Kermit Roosevelt, the son of President Teddy Roosevelt, on a yacht to the Pacific Ocean to collect information on Japanese installments during the War. Upon inheriting his fortune at the age of 20, Astor dropped out of Harvard and dedicated his life to public service. By the time he appeared on *Forbes*' list of America's richest men, Astor was estimated to be worth $75,000,000.

The OSS placed its people in position of power around the world, expanding the Rothschild intelligence network and back channels. One agent, Allen Dulles, who was drawn from a family of diplomats and international attorneys, recruited over 100 agents in Germany including lawyers, businessmen, and labor leaders.[xxvi] Dulles was later appointed to head Central Intelligence under President Dwight Eisenhower. Another OSS agent, William Casey, became Director of Central Intelligence under President Ronald Reagan. The theatrical Julia Child joined the OSS as an assistant to Donovan before being given her own television cooking show. Other prominent OSS agents include Arthur Goldberg, a future Supreme Court Justice; Ralph Bunche, Ambassador to the United Nations; and Frederick Mayer, a German-born Jew who posed as a German officer to gather intelligence that helped defeat Nazi Germany.[xxvii]

Reflecting the close relationship between the media and intelligence community, Lawrence "Larry" Lowman, a CBS Vice President who had worked on the technical aspects of the network's radio programs, was tapped to join the OSS Communications Branch to transmit secret communications among OSS locations.[xxviii] During the war, the OSS trained Germans and Austrians for missions inside Germany – and recruiting exiled communists and Socialist party members, labor activists, anti-Nazi prisoners-of-war, Nazi scientists, German and Jewish refugees, Chinese, Arabs, French, all of whom became interwoven within the fabric of the American Deep State, which secretly wielded influence on the American federal government on behalf of powerful private interests.

Through the OSS, communists were able to move into positions of power within the federal government, helping the British Crown and its agents weaken the country from within, as revealed in Aleksandr Dugin's *The Foundations of Geopolitics: the Geopolitical Future of Russia.* Communists, he wrote, should "spread anti-Americanism everywhere," and make the United States "the scapegoat" of the world's ills. A leader of the National Bolshevik Party, Dugin promoted the "use of (Russian) special services within the borders of the United States to fuel instability and separatism" and provoke "Afro-American racists." The book advocated introducing "geopolitical disorder into internal American activity, encouraging ... separatism, ethnic, social, and racial conflicts, (and) actively supporting all dissident movements – extremists, racists, and sectarian groups (to destabilize) internal political processes in the United States (while) simultaneously (supporting) isolationist tendencies in American politics."

The military was skeptical of the apparatus Donovan had built[xxix] as his reports were often unfocused and lacking in substance. Further, the OSS operated within the shadows of society, engaging in subversive, and at times, illegal activities while somehow remaining above the law.

The federal government initially resisted the network's covert operations, which involved "making things happen without allowing it to be known that the United States was the instigator."[xxx] The agents were trouble makers who excelled at old world strategies of espionage, propaganda, sabotage, false flag events, smear campaigns, psychological warfare, subversion, assassinations, political manipulation, dirty tricks, guerrilla attacks, spontaneous riots, and other unconventional warfare strategies designed to influence public opinion, subvert society, and advance elite policy goals, changing America within a span of decades from a moral nation into an ethical cesspool.

Before the group was dismantled, the OSS set up operations in Istanbul, Turkey to host spy networks for both the Axis and Allies powers, reflecting elite involvement in both sides of the war through which they stood to profit. The railroads, which connected central Asia with Europe, placed Turkey at "the crossroads of intelligence gathering."[xxxi] Through Turkey, the OSS sought to infiltrate the Ottoman and Austro-Hungarian Empires. By the end of World War II, the OSS was running a private intelligence service out of an office in Wall Street, "using some of the biggest names in American business."[xxxii]

While working in intelligence gathering, Starr reportedly recruited an OSS Captain by the name of Duncan Lee to serve as general counsel for AIG. While Mao Zedong led the People's Liberation Army through Shanghai in 1949, Starr relocated AIG headquarters from China to New York City.

President Harry Truman shut down the OSS operation after uncovering "allegations of a wide range of alleged OSS misbehavior." He also concluded that Donovan's proposed peacetime intelligence activities stood to violate the rights of ordinary American citizens. "I'd rather have a young lieutenant with enough guts to disobey a direct order than a colonel too regimented to think for himself," Donovan complained.

The CIA, a civilian foreign intelligence agency, was established in 1947 to succeed the OSS. In 1974, Vice President Nelson Rockefeller led the President's Commission on CIA Activities within the United States, otherwise known as the Rockefeller Commission, after the *New York Times* reported that the CIA had engaged in illegal activities against U.S. citizens, including opening mail, domestic surveillance, and experimenting with mind control through LSD and MK Ultra.

The Commission reaffirmed that the Constitution protected U.S. citizens from unnecessary government intrusion and that "violent change, or forcing a change of government by the stealthily action of enemies, foreign or domestic, is contrary to our Constitutional system." Reflecting a pre-September 11, 2001 mindset, the Commission concluded that "the mere invocation of national security does not grant unlimited power to the government....(and) the preservation of individual liberties within the United States requires limitations or restrictions on intelligence." However, Rockefeller was quick to assert that the "drawing of reasonable lines – where legitimate intelligence needs end and erosion of Constitutional government begins – is difficult."

The Commission argued for increased surveillance within the United States on grounds that "intelligence is information gathered for policymakers in government which illuminates the range of choices available to them and enables them to exercise judgment." Yet, that information was available principally to elites and their networks which sought to have the government serve them and their business interests, providing them access to information to which duly elected officials, including the President, were not even privy. Information gathered with regards to "(foreign) military capabilities, subversive activities, economic conditions, political developments, scientific and technological progress, and social activities and conditions" could be provided to "the President and the political, military, and other governmental leaders according to their needs," Rockefeller said.

While promoting an expansion of intelligence operations within the United States, Rockefeller conceded that "we cannot ignore the invasion of the privacy and security rights of Americans by foreign countries or their agents." Surveillance must be increased, he said, as "the United States remains the principal intelligence target of the communist bloc." The communists, he said, "invest large sums of money, personnel and sophisticated technology in collecting information within the United States on our military capabilities, our weapons systems, our defense structure, and our social divisions. The communists seek to penetrate our intelligence services, to compromise our law enforcement agencies, and to recruit as their agents United States citizens holding sensitive government and industry jobs."

The Commission estimated that over 500,000 intelligence forces worldwide were working on behalf of communists and that the number of communists working within the federal government had tripled since 1960. As would later become clear, the same corporate interests that had warned the United States about encroaching communism were financing or otherwise aiding and abetting its rise; they were also transferring technology to enemies of the United States that would later be used to subvert American interests and violate the rights of the U.S. citizens, tactics that increased the power of elites and enriched them further through government contracts.

While Nelson Rockefeller was exploring the limits of surveillance, his brother, Laurance Rockefeller, was providing venture capital through Venrock Associates to help "entrepreneurs build some of the world's most disruptive, successful companies, (giving) entrepreneurs the unfair advantage needed to win, and win big." Among its clients were Intel, Apple, and a number of tech and aerospace companies that were making inroads into Russia, China, and Israeli markets.

By the end of his career, Starr, a humble man who grew up on an Indian reservation, controlled nearly 150 owned and affiliated insurance and insurance agency companies in over 100 countries. The company he built would go on to write close to $700,000,000 in premiums each year and cover many billions of dollars in underwriting exposures. "You have to have worries, but you're better off having them in a Cadillac than in a rickshaw," Starr said. At its peak, AIG obtained a market capitalization of $180,000,000,000, making it "the largest insurance and financial services company in history."[xxxiii]

As head of AIG, the Starr Foundation reported, Starr "surrounded himself with promising youngsters whose bounce helped him feel alive. They were invited to visit his estate in Brewster, New York and many were given personal scholarships to help them in the world. Starr used to call this form of philanthropy 'corrupting.' He enjoyed overwhelming the minds and hearts of young people with opportunity. One of his protégés said, 'It was such a luxurious corruption that no young person of limited means would ever think of refusing. Many other people wished they were included in his life of corrupted minds'." As the Starr Foundation affirmed, Starr's career "was the career of a man who believed that good business was no more than the sum of capable men doing what they could do well in a way that became them best." His nephew, Ken Starr, would serve as independent counsel to investigate the Clinton's Whitewater land deal and the Lewinsky scandal, reporting in prurient detail the President's sexual dalliances while turning a blind eye to the Chinese money that funded the Clinton's political campaigns as the Clintons and their globalist allies colluded with elites to collapse the American economy to make way for a new world order led by Communist China.

As Starr retired, he selected Maurice "Hank" Greenberg to succeed him at AIG, though he would later characterize his successor as "greedy." Greenberg acquired an impressive array of elite credentials after having presided over the Federal Reserve Bank of New York, the New York Stock Exchange, the Asia Society, and the Nixon Center. As Trustee of Rockefeller University, Greenberg became a member of the Trilateral Commission, which promoted the elite agenda of integrating regional markets throughout the world under a global structure managed by a world government. Greenberg was eventually nominated to serve as Director of Central Intelligence and referenced as a source for a Council of Foreign Relations task force on intelligence reform.

The Deep State looked after its own, helping its members become rich and powerful. AIG created a strategic advisory venture team with Kissinger Associates and the Blackstone Group, a private equity firm, "to provide financial advisory services to corporations seeking high level independent strategic advice." Blackstone acted as an adviser to AIG during the 2007-2008 financial crisis, helping the federal government support the notion that AIG was "too big to fail." AIG received $182,000,000,000 through the Troubled Asset Relief Program, with taxpayers reportedly losing nearly $30,000,000,000 in the deal. Instead of forcing AIG's creditors to take a hit, the Treasury Department, which was run by a revolving door of executives from elite investment banks, insisted that the company be paid in full.

Following the terrorist attacks of September 11, 2001, AIG lobbied for legislation that guaranteed federal support for insurance claims stemming from future terrorist attacks in order to limit its own liability. In November of 2001, Sen. John McCain who had received $40,000 from AIG between 1990 and 2006, introduced the Terrorism Insurance Act, which served this very purpose.

The intelligence apparatus Starr and Donovan created proved immensely useful during the Cold War, enabling the federal government to gather timely information on the Soviets which enabled them to subvert communist plots. This feat was not difficult to accomplish considering that the network they had created had been involved in them in the first place. The amount of money the federal government would spend on defense contracts during this period was astronomical.

***

Is nothing sacred to the elites? The answer is no. Not even the church was spared its corrupting influence. The Catholic Church, which harbored globalist aspirations of its own, was poised to extinguish communism. Where the communists were materialistic, the Vatican was a powerful defender of Christian morals and ethics, with millions of devoted followers throughout the world adhering to its moral and spiritual prescriptions. If the rebellious Protestants diluted their political force by splitting from the Vatican to cultivate a personal relationship with God through Jesus and by choosing to think for themselves instead of following a falliblePope, the Catholic Church served as God's material representative on earth through a phalanx of nuns and priests who were supported by Jesuit schools.

Somewhere along the way, the Catholic church began to rot from within. Instead of providing moral guidance for the people, it provided moral cover for elites. To this day, the French and British absolutely hate each other, a hatred stemming from longstanding dynastic battles. In the 1800s, French Emperor Napoleon Bonaparte challenged the British East India Company, an agent of the British Crown, for control of Europe. He resisted efforts to make France indebted, and therefore controlled, by international bankers. "When a government is dependent upon bankers for money, they and not the leaders of the government control the situation, since the hand that gives is above the hand that takes," Napoleon said. "Money has no motherland; financiers are without patriotism and without decency; their sole object is gain."

It would not be long before the Catholic Church was infiltrated by Rothschild agents who used the Vatican as moral cover for power and money grabs. "In an era of globalization, it is key to remember that the Catholic Church has been a global institution for centuries," said Francis Rooney, former U.S. Ambassador to the Vatican.[xxxiv] While Rothschild was financing the British, freedom loving President Thomas Jefferson agreed to the Louisiana Purchase so that the United States could expand westward across the North American continent while providing Napoleon the capital he needed to resist the British East India Company's conquest of Europe. America was already pushing back against the Crown's imperialistic designs, leading elites to double down on their efforts to conquer the country from within.

During the Napoleonic Wars, Rothschild established a network of couriers and agents, upon which the OSS would later be based, that provided timely intelligence to enhance the family's ability to profit and gain diplomatic leverage. The Rothschilds reportedly began loaning money to the Holy See in 1832 for intelligence and other purposes. Napoleon was defeated decisively at the Battle of Waterloo after Nathan Mayer Rothschild shipped gold bullion to British armies led by the Duke of Wellington.

During the Second World War, the OSS opened lines of communication with the Vatican under the guise of fighting communism. "Donovan realized during the war that the Catholic Church, with its own network of religion spread wide and deep around the world, was a valuable resource for the spy agency," U.S. Ambassador to the Vatican Francis Rooney wrote in <u>The Global Vatican</u>. "This was the start of an important alliance between the Vatican and America's intelligence." President Harry S. Truman concluded that "the Soviets and their communist associates must be halted, particularly after the Soviets acquired the atomic bomb and Mao Zedong seized control of China," he wrote. "America needed religion to prevail. Above all, it needed the Roman Catholic Church."

Truman also reached out to the Federal Council of Churches (later renamed the National Council of Churches), which was founded in 1908 to unite the disparate Protestant denominations against communism after this ideology emerged as an existential threat to Christianity and its values. Gradually the National Council of Churches and the World Council of Churches were infiltrated by communists who encouraged the church to march towards "a visible unity in one faith and one eucharistic fellowship." As Willem Adolph Visser T. Hooft, the Secretary General of the World Council of Churches said,[xxxv] "The League of Churches was to become a union of all churches on faith and order as the final purpose of the League of Nations...The dream dreamt by so many philosophers, the dream of international order, based on law and justice, seemed ... to become a political reality."

To this end, churches were encouraged to consolidate their resources by joining together. Once this task was accomplished, hierarchies were established above the local churches, allowing distant bureaucrats to dictate and dilute doctrine, referencing the *Gospel of John* as their authority. Globalists claimed that it was God's will for the churches to come together as one based upon Jesus' prayer that "for those who will believe in me through their message, that all of them may be as one, Father, just as you are in me and I am in you." (*John 17:26*) The union of churches was intended to serve as a foundation for the political union of nations.

An FBI researcher by the name of Edgar C. Bundy wrote that the globalists interpreted Jesus' call for spiritual unity to mean materialistic unity. Having worked as an intelligence officer during the Second World War, Bundy was privy to elite plans to align Christian doctrine with communism in order to usher in a new world order. In addition to predicting the fall of China to communism, he warned that globalists were attempting to eliminate differences among the Christian denominations to establish a spiritual foundation for a one world government. "If one were to look into the historic confessions of faith, catechisms, or creeds of these denominations which come together, one would find doctrinal beliefs which would forbid them to come together in such a manner," he wrote.[xxxvi] "But when these churches were so thoroughly captured by liberals who led them into the fellowship of the Federal Council of Churches, doctrine was no longer of any concern. The idea of getting together, regardless of belief, was the primary thing."

The Kremlin-backed Russian Orthodox Church joined the WCC in 1966 to prevent it from becoming "a single front of Protestant churches against atheism and communism (to) show the Western Christians the light of Orthodoxy."[xxxvii] "The light of Orthodoxy was communism. " As Bundy observed, Bolshevik agitators and priests took over the Russian Orthodox Church in 1922 through the Living Church Movement.[xxxviii] The movement was "based on the idea of reinterpreting the teachings of Christ and the Apostles in such a way as to serve communist ends....(For example), there is a portion of the

Bible which tells how Christ chased the money changers out of the temple. This would be interpreted as meaning that Christ was anti-capitalist or against moneyed people! The general idea was to move from the spiritual concept to the materialist one and to make the church an instrument of social strife, to substitute the materialistic social (justice) gospel for the supernatural salvation gospel.... Materialistic, humanistic, and rationalistic philosophies were substituted for the divine historic message and mission of the church."

The origins of the ecumenical movement (which sought to merge the Christian denominations and the religions of the world into one) trace to the United Kingdom. As Europe smoldered in the ashes of the World Wars, John Mott, a community organizer who led the World Student Christian Federation, convened the World Missionary Conference in Edinburgh, Scotland to preserve peace and lay down the "marching orders that (involved) members of every Protestant church around the world ... to (unite) Christianity."[xxxix]

In 1948, Mott was enlisted to establish the World Council of Churches. Standard Oil founder John D. Rockefeller donated $1,000,000 to Mott to fund a WCC Commission on International Relations "to stimulate the churches of all nations to a more vigorous expression of the demands of the Christians conscience in relation to the political policies of government."

Among Mott's greatest supporters were not the ordinary, humble people whom Jesus championed, but the moneyed elites who exploited them. "To ask money of a man for the purposes of the world-wide Kingdom of God is not to ask him a favor – it is to give him a superb opportunity of investing his personality in eternal shares," Mott said.[xl] As an "apostle of unity," Mott convinced progressive Protestant denominations to support "a vision of worldwide Christianity based on concepts they believed Christians around the world could agree on and work together to implement."[xli] The organization of the WCC was modeled after Rockefeller's Standard Oil.[xlii]

A sign of things to come, in 1917, the Federal Council of Churches referenced Jesus as the "first socialist."[xliii] The President of Harding College observed that socialists were advocating "the extensive use of taxation to reduce inequalities in income. This advocacy is contrary to the fundamental principles of the American way of life and our historic American concept of taxation. Taxation in America was conceived as a fair and sound method of financing government – and for no other purpose, but socialists long ago found it to be their handiest instrument for achieving abolition of private property and the subjugation of a people."[xliv]

The Federal Council of Churches then published a pamphlet entitled "Social Ideals of the Churches," to promote the "subordination of ... the profit motive" and called for "a wider and fairer distribution of the wealth," said Dr. William Patron, a co-secretary at the WCC.[xlv] Referencing the ecumenical movement, Secretary of State John Foster Dulles told the *New York Times* after World War II that, "We are aiming for a top organization, international in character, to coordinate the thinking and actions of Protestant denominations through their national organizations. We will attempt to make it do for religion what labor does through the World Federation of Trade Unions."[xlvi]

By 2012, the WCC claimed to speak for over 600,000,000 Christians in 150 countries, including 520,000 local congregations and nearly 500,000 pastors and priests. With the WCC setting the agenda, church ministers encouraged congregations to put their faith into action by marching for social justice, open borders, income redistribution, socialized medicine, entitlement programs, and federal aid, spurring a bonanza of government contracts which redistributed wealth from the middle classes to the rich while professing concern for the poor.

As socialism spread through the congregations, Christians perceived that the spiritual core of the church was being hollowed out, leading many to abandon the pews. "The gulf between those who make national decisions and those who sit in the pews (is deep)," Bundy wrote.[xlvii] "The men and women in the pews know nothing whatsoever about the National Council of Churches and its workings. The National Council claims to speak for Protestants on the United Nations, yet these questions have never been submitted to the people for a vote, nor have the people ever been consulted by ballot as to whether or not they even wanted membership in the Federal, National, or World Council of Churches."

The Occupy Wall Street Movement, which launched in 2011, encouraged people to take to the streets to preach the social gospel through congregation-based community organizations. Throngs of OWS activists descended upon New York to demand that wealth be redistributed from the haves to the have nots. "We are the 99 percent," the activists proclaimed as they marched through the Manhattan financial district parroting communist talking points. The Riverside Church, which had received donations from John D. Rockefeller, Jr., donated tents for the protesters and fed them deviled eggs.[xlviii]

OWS activists congregated around Zuccotti Park, which was established in 1968 by U.S. Steel, and conceived nearly a century earlier by J.P Morgan, steel magnate Andrew Carnegie, and billionaire oil tycoon John D. Rockefeller. The group promised to form a "revolutionary force that, with your active involvement, might reshape how power and meaning flow in the 21st century." While claiming to be a grassroots movement, according to *Activistcash.com*, a number of progressive groups, including, for example, the Tides Foundation and Tides Center, which receive money from the Rockefeller Brothers Fund and the Rockefeller Foundation, have contributed to its operations.

With OWS activists taking to the streets to agitate for justice, the National Council of Churches encouraged the federal government to "invest in a social safety net" through a Faithful Budget. "To get the deficit under control, the federal government needs more money," the NCC said. Churches were assigned the task of distributing income more equitably. After the federal government bailed out Wall Street, the NCC argued that the $787,000,000,000 stimulus package "may not be large enough."

As Americans struggled to pay their bills, the NCC advocated opening borders to a deluge of unskilled immigrants who were willing to take jobs for lower wages than that which Americans needed to support themselves. The government was expected to help the poor immigrants make ends meet by providing them taxpayer-supported subsidized housing, disability payments, child support, free schooling, and free medical services. The church argued that new immigrants should enjoy these privileges over the native born on grounds that the immigrant poor and dispossessed were among "the least of these," just like Jesus and Mary.

The churches encouraged their congregants and the federal government to give immigrants an extravagant welcome. In the interests of "greater economic fairness," the recent immigrants should receive benefits denied to veterans who had sacrificed life and limb on behalf of the country. The proposed "Faithful Budget" required the United States to "fully fund" global agencies and initiatives, including the U.S. Agency for International Development and the Global

Partnerships for Migration and Refugee Assistance.

While communism was seeping into the American Protestant churches, the CIA reported that "to avoid upsetting Catholics, communists would initially attempt to be more Catholic than the Vatican."[xlix] In a letter to the Pope dated November 21, 1946, President Harry S. Truman wrote that the American people prayed that "all moral forces of the world will unite ... in an enduring world order." The Truman Administration believed that the Vatican could assist "by securing the influence of the Holy See to mobilize 300,000,000 Catholics throughout the world in support of (American) objectives and to some extent, influencing the 38 governments who now maintain diplomatic relations in the Holy See," Rooney wrote. "It is well known that the Holy See is vigorously engaged in the growing fight against communism." Within the United States, the Catholics would become its most passionate and vocal critics.

In an effort to cultivate a close relationship with the Holy See, President Harry S. Truman instructed the State Department to nominate an ambassador to the Vatican, recommending a leading anti-communist, Allen Dulles, who had served as Donovan's right hand man at the OSS. Allen had presided over the CIA while his brother, John Foster Dulles, served as Secretary of State. Both brothers were dedicated globalists. The Dulles appointment did not go forward, however. As sons of ordained Jesuits, the Dulles brothers "oversaw overt and covert aspects of American foreign policy that (were aimed) at halting communism"[l] while their allies were spreading it. "Defeating communism was not just a matter of realpolitik," Rooney said. "it was a moral imperative."

In 1953, William Colby, a former OSS agent, took over the CIA office in Rome to "demonstrate that we could help our friends and frustrate our foes (through) considerable sharing of information" and a "modicum of coordination" between the CIA and Vatican."[li] As Rooney acknowledged, "dealing with the Holy See afforded the United States an avenue for the moderate and careful exchange of information and opinions." It would not be long before the Vatican and globalist elites were speaking from the same script. Among the Ambassadors to the Vatican was Ann Clare Boothe Luce, the wife of Henry Luce, whom C.V. Starr had befriended in China. With the OSS and its agents providing intelligence that helped defeat Hitler, Boothe was on hand to witness the liberation of Nazi concentration camps.

The Catholic Church provided the soft power required to lead Christendom into the new world. After the World Wars claimed millions of lives, the Pope appeared before the UN General Assembly to appeal for an end to war. By 1964, the Holy See had acquired Permanent Observer status within the United Nations, creating the perception of neutrality while the Vatican advocated for more global control to prevent war and fight communism. President Ronald Reagan worked diligently with the Pope to "hasten the dissolution of the communist empire."[lii] He also praised the " moral and political influence the Pope and Vatican exercised throughout the world on behalf of Western values."

"The early decades of the 20th century found the (Catholic church) in alignment with right wing regimes," Rooney wrote. "In the mid 1960s, this changed in some areas as the movement of liberation theology spread throughout the local clergy. Followers of liberation theology (drew upon communist principles to design policies which they claimed would) help the poor, alleviate hunger, push for justice, and stand up to despots, but in so doing they drew the church into domestic politics. The pastoral mission of the church became too closely aligned with secular government."

In 2002, UN Secretary General Kofi Annan invited the Vatican to apply for full membership in the global organization, but the Vatican declined on grounds that "membership would detract rather than support its status," Rooney wrote. "By maintaining its status as Permanent Observer, the Holy See could continue to advocate for its own universal agenda by exerting influence. By staying above the fray – the deal making, the dog fighting and preserving its universality and moral authority, the Holy See maintained its bias for neutrality, morality, and truth. This is precisely the source of its soft power."

Since 1965, the Catholic Church has participated in joint working groups with the World Council of Churches to "regularly discuss issues of common interest and promote cooperation." Through this relationship, the Vatican and WCC have wielded influence on the world stage through moral appeals. Given the lure of profits through government contracts, Catholic and Protestant churches have teamed up with Jewish synagogues to unleash the tap on public funds to help resettle and provide taxpayer-support for endless waves of refugees and poor immigrants to Western Europe and the United States as part of a global income redistribution and resettlement scheme.

In 2016, with immigrants flooding across borders, the United Nations Declaration for Refugees and Migrants declared migration to be "a human right," regardless of the financial, social, or political impact of the countries of destination. Citizens of recipient countries were not only not consulted on the matter, but their concerns were consistently ignored. At the same time, they were expected to foot the bill and sacrifice to accommodate the newcomers.

Despite the elites' virtue signaling and professions of concern for the poor, the globalist legacy has told an entirely different story. Millions of people have lost their lives, and millions more, their fortunes and their countries to communism and other income redistribution schemes. At heart, globalists were never interested in redistributing the wealth from the haves to the have nots, but in fleecing the haves so that they could have even more.

***

The British East India Company helped project the British Crown's influence into the United States political establishment through Yale, a university established by Eli Yale, who acquired his fortune through the opium trade. Among the recipients of opium money was Yale University, which attracted the children of elites, many of whom were connected to the East India Company. By and large, these were not the children of the professional classes or of the church communities but the children of mercenaries, pirates, and societal parasites, a self-perpetuating elite who sought to reinforce its privilege and amass greater wealth through public money, crony capitalism, and income redistribution schemes they devised to plunder the public purse.

With Brown Brothers Harriman & Co. serving as Trustee, the Russell Sage Foundation established a secret society at Yale called Skull & Bones whose alumni went on to assume positions of power in American society, including, for example, Sen. John Kerry, Bush dynasty patriarch Prescott Bush; President George H.W. Bush; and President George W. Bush. Reflecting the secret path to riches through the Indian tribes, Prescott was reputed to have raided the tomb of Apache Chief Geronimo, absconded with the skull, and showcased his trophy in the Skull & Bones crypt.

The World Wars proved immensely profitable for the elites.

Public funds were quickly released for war contracts and then on infrastructure contracts to rebuild the war torn nations afterward. As the British *Guardian* newspaper reported in 2004, Prescott Bush served as director and shareholder in companies that profited through financial relationships with Nazi Germany.[liii] While the United States was at war with Hitler's Germany, the Bush patriarch was providing comfort to the enemy. "Even after America had entered the war and when there was already significant information about the Nazis' plans and policies, (Prescott Bush) worked for and profited from companies closely involved with the very German businesses that financed Hitler's rise to power," the *Guardian* reported. "It has also been suggested that the money he made from these dealings helped to establish the Bush family fortune and set up its political dynasty."

The Bush patriarch's employer at the time was Brown Brothers Harriman, a private investment bank whose assets were valued at $5,600,000,000,000 as of 2017 and which had deep and longstanding ties with the nation's leading industrialists and bankers, employing such notables as Federal Reserve Chairman Alan Greenspan who married NBC's senior foreign policy correspondent Andrea Mitchell; and William Averell Harriman, a Secretary of Commerce under President Harry S. Truman, who attended Yale University.

During the Administration of President Franklin Delano Roosevelt, Harriman worked at the National Recovery Administration, an agency established during the New Deal to eliminate competition by bringing industry, labor, and government together to establish terms for "fair business" practices.

Harriman also helped coordinate the Lend-Lease program, which provided $50,100,000,000 in wartime support to the UK, China, and Soviet Union, and other Allied nations, using taxpayer money to purchase and distribute military equipment, food, and oil. In addition to serving as Ambassador the Soviet Union, Harriman became a keen supporter of George Kennan's policy of containment of the Soviet Union while fellow Bush bonesman and elite U.S. corporate interests helped finance its expansion.

As Secretary of Commerce, Harriman coordinated the Marshall Plan which released $12,000,000,000 in economic assistance to help rebuild war-torn Europe, remove trade barriers, and modernize its industry. While the Marshall Plan served the purpose of containing the Soviet Union and expanding U.S. influence – and by extension, its hegemony – into Europe, the nation's leading corporations acquired market share while American citizens acquired debt.

An economist from Stanford University's Hoover Institute, Anthony Sutton who authored <u>Wall Street and the Bolshevik Revolution</u> and <u>FDR and the Wall Street and the Rise of Hitler,</u> reported that members of Skull & Bones had built the communist movements in China and given aid to the Soviet communists and then played each other against each other and the United States in order to drum up profits for Wall Street. Even more devastating, he alleged in <u>National Suicide: Military Aid to the Soviet Union</u> that the Cold War had "not been fought to restrain communism" since the United States was financing the USSR and either directly or indirectly arming both sides in Korea and Vietnam in order to generate multi-billion armaments contracts.[liv]

Through the World Wars, the Cold War, and then the War on Terrorism, corporate America had reportedly pitted countries and ideologies against each other to generate profits for themselves while weakening the United States through debt, cultural subversion, and an erosion of civil liberties, all for the purpose of consolidating the world's wealth and power into the hands of the few.

The United States was exceptional by virtue of the fluidity of its class system and its fealty to God. Americans could expect to succeed or fail through their own initiative, talents, and drive. Yet, as a result of the reckless, self-serving actions of the elites, the American dream was increasingly falling out of reach for many. Elites, threatened by the creativity and entrepreneurial spirit of the people, worked to undermine them, lower their educational standards, limit their access to information, and misinform them through fake news while introducing chaos and instability into their society and rivals to their jobs. They also fomenting societal dissent so that the public exhausted its energies and resources fighting each other rather than addressing the betrayals of the political and corporate classes.

Sutton concluded that based upon his research, Wall Street had financed and backed the Bolshevik Revolution to undermine Russia as an economic competitor so that it would be a "captive market and a technical colony to be exploited by a few high powered American financiers and the corporations under their control." He also observed that this same network had financed the rise of Adolph Hitler and President Franklin Delano Roosevelt, who advanced "corporate socialism" as part of a "long range program of nurturing collectivism" to guarantee "a monopoly on the acquisition of wealth."

By the end of the World War, American elites would set their sights on the profits they could derive through the vast, untapped Chinese market. In 1968 as Richard Nixon sought the Presidential nomination, he said, "Taking the long view, we simply cannot afford to leave China forever outside the family of nations."

***

For the rest of the world, China was a foreign, distant, and exotic land whose people spoke a complex, almost indecipherable foreign language and whose culture was steeped in traditions that had been nurtured over centuries with limited exposure to outsiders. The globalists salivated over the wealth they stood to make by exploiting China. They approached the Chinese not as a people whose culture they sought to preserve nor as equals. Instead, they pushed opium and other drugs on them to weaken and confuse the people while fattening their own pocketbooks. The elite infiltration into Chinese society was gradual, but devastating, both for China and the United States.

While John D. Rockefeller was quietly making investments in Indian Country, he was selling kerosene to the Chinese and endowing Chinese missions.[lv] By 1933, the Rockefeller Foundation had invested more than $37,000,000 in the Orient.[lvi] Among the priorities of the Rockefeller Foundation were building an effective agricultural economy and "stimulating Chinese leadership." Rockefeller efforts helped establish the North China Council for Rural Reconstruction, which promoted university departments and academic research, similar to those in the United States which produced reports that were used to appeal for government contracts and separate taxpayers from their money and erode their rights.[lvii] The program ended with the Japanese invasion of 1937.

"Despite its lack of overt success, the Rural Reconstruction program (is) credited with providing a model for the subsequent community development initiatives of the Rockefeller Foundation and other international aid organizations, (like) the U.S. technical assistance program that eventually became the Agency for International Development (USAID)," the Rockefeller Foundation reported.[lviii] "The sentiments that my grandfather and grandmother and other relatives had for China (are) very positive feeling for the country, passed through the generations to all of us," Rockefeller Brothers Fund Chairman of the Board Richard Rockefeller told reporters. "So China in a way wasn't such an unfamiliar place it might been to a lot of Americans."

As elites positioned themselves to tap into the Chinese market, the Yale campus newspaper revealed that Yale University and Skull & Bones created Communist China.[lix] The university had also educated, trained, and sponsored Mao Zedong, the Communist agitator who led the Chinese Cultural Revolution. The People's Republic of China centralized control in the country so that international bankers and corporations could acquire the resources and opportunities they needed to develop China through government fiat and public money. Through China, the elites aspired to rule the new world order. Under Mao's leadership, millions of innocent people lost their lives, just as they had done in the Soviet Union.

The OSS was on hand to train Mao's Red Army, with Donovan personally briefing Operational Group members in Bethesda, Maryland before their departure to China in 1945. The OSS established bases around the world from East Asia to training camps in Catoctin Mountain Park, the location of Camp David.

Yale in China was founded by Yale Divinity School, which offered a "rich ecumenical setting... (to) cultivate the skills necessary for professional ministry in a post-denominational world."[lx] In 1919, Mao was introduced to Communist theory in a Marxist Study Group in Shanghai; the Yale Student Union invited him to create a Yale campus in China. Under the advisement of his mentors, Mao promoted "Thought Reorientation" as editor of their journal.[lxi] "Without Yale, support of Mao Zedong may never have risen from obscurity to command China," Yale Professor Jonathan Spence said.

Through his association with the university, Mao was able to establish a Chinese branch of the Communist Party. Since he had neither the funds nor real estate to achieve this task, "Yale stepped in by (renting) him three rooms (in) the Cultural Book Store" through which Mao published such titles as An Introduction to Marx's Capital, A Study of the New Russia, and The Soviet System in China. "Maos's reputation grew, " the newspaper reported. From this base he was able to organize several branch stores." The profits were reinvested in a Socialist Youth Corps and the Communist Party.

Given the success of his efforts, Mao became a delegate to the First Congress of the Chinese Communist Party, which financed the Socialist Youth Corps and the Communist Party, providing him a platform for the launch of the Communist Movement in China.

As Yale's hospitals, intelligence networks, and agents infiltrated China on behalf of the Anglo-American establishment, the university collaborated with the OSS at the direction of Reuben Holder. A loyal member of Skull & Bones, Holder installed Maoists into power; they, in turn, became the largest opium producers. At the same time, the secret society and its affiliated networks gave financial aid to communists within the Soviet union with the view to bankrupting and breaking the back of Russia and its satellite states to prevent free enterprise from flourishing there so that state-sponsored corporations created by and for the Anglo-American establishment could dominate those markets, reap the profits, and control their governments. Back channel networks affiliated with the OSS and Skull & Bones worked with the Chinese to defeat the Soviets and Japanese during the Second World War.

Instead of being perceived as a threat by Western corporate elites, Mao was heartily welcomed. Writing for Henry Luce's *Time* magazine, for example, David Rockefeller, the Chairman of the Board of Chase Manhattan Bank, paid homage to "the real and pervasive dedication of Chairman Mao to Marxist principles," conceding that "whatever the price of the Chinese Revolution, it has obviously succeeded in producing more dedicated administration...and community of purpose."[lxii] Having traveled to China with the Chase group, Rockefeller praised "the enormous social advantages of China," which he attributed to "the singleness of ideology and purpose....We, on our part, are faced with the realization that we have largely ignored a country with ¼ of the world's population....The social experiment in China under Chairman Mao's leadership is one of the most important and successful in human history."

Perceiving the threat Mao posed to China, Chiang Kai-shek and his Nationalist Party took over the Chinese government and forced the Yale infiltrators out, only to retreat to Taiwan. While the United States government paid lip service to Taiwan, the actions of the U.S. political establishment demonstrated that the loyalties and interests of global elites were aligned with those of the Communist Chinese. To cite but one example, Yale's newspaper reveled in an American-

Chinese communiqué that announced U.S. troop withdrawal from Taiwan with unbounded glee: "Yale scholars seemed pleased and gratified that the United States has chosen to diminish its role in what the experts consistently referred to as a Chinese problem....American troops never belonged in Taiwan to begin with and...Taiwan has always been doomed because it refused to surrender its claim to authority over mainland China."

That withdrawal came during the Administration of President Richard Nixon, who was credited with restoring and normalizing America's relationship with China. Tapped to help implement his China policy was George H.W. Bush, a bonesman who served as Nixon's *de facto* Ambassador to Taiwan. Another notable bonesman, William F. Buckley, the author of <u>God and Man at Yale</u> who was credited with launching the modern conservative movement, accompanied Nixon on a trip to China. Secretary of State Henry Kissinger, an ambitious academic affiliated with the Rockefeller-funded Council of Foreign Relations, who served on the Board of Trustees of the Rockefeller Brothers Fund, helped restore relations with China while advancing foreign policy that would be devastating to the United States and the world at large.

As Kissinger opened the door to the East, David Rockefeller was quick to convene a meeting at the penthouse of Chase Manhattan Bank to forge strategy. The men met with the senior executives of close to 300 major U.S. corporations and the founders of China International Trust Investment Corporation, a state-owned investment company of the People's Republic of China established in 1979 with the approval of Deng Xiaoping.

The National Committee on U.S.-China Relations opened its doors at the library of the Church Center of the United Nations building in New York with financial assistance from John D. Rockefeller III and the Sloan Foundation, as a public relations offensive to foster greater openness and receptivity among the American people to China, stating "to fulfill its goals, the National Committee must reach all segments of American society from the laymen to the specialists. It must also keep abreast of continuing developments in China to tap available sources of knowledge."

Among those who would serve on the National Committee's Board were Henry Kissinger and Maurice "Hank" Greenberg. Through the back channels the elites had forged during the two World Wars, they would incrementally attempt to weaken the United States so that China could emerged as leader of the new world order. The elites in turn expected to make record profits through the vast, untapped Chinese markets on the backs of American taxpayers, reducing standard of living, freedoms, and standing in the world of ordinary citizens. If opening the doors to the communists wasn't bad enough, Kissinger would set the United States on a path to perdition by seeking to constrain its power and that of other countries through entangled foreign engagements that served corporate, over national, interests.

IV.

Oil Diplomacy and Subversion

As elites implemented a carefully crafted agenda to subvert the United States, principled insiders came forward to warn the American people. One such man was Ken Fromm, the Chief Operating Officer of Atlantic Richfield.

While exploring oil in Alaska, Fromm confided in his pastor, Lindsey Williams, that a pool had been discovered around Prudhoe Bay that was large enough to make the United States energy independent for generations. Despite this miraculous finding, powerful forces within the Nixon Administration blocked the oil companies from extracting it until the price of oil reached $150-$200/barrel, a prospect that stood to devastate the economy by destroying the livelihood of ordinary citizens and dramatically increasing the cost of living and doing business within the United States all the while generating untold wealth for elites.

A faith-filled man who loved God and country, Williams exposed the agenda in a book entitled The Non-Energy Crisis, which demonstrated that the United States was not facing an energy shortage. The oil fields in Alaska were larger than those in Saudi Arabia and could have sustained the United States for at least a hundred years, he said.[lxiii] At the time this decision was made, Nixon's Secretary of State, Henry Kissinger, was embarking on a strategy of oil diplomacy throughout the world in which he sought to curtail the independence of nations in the interests of globalism by enmeshing countries in "linkages" that would render them interdependent and unable to act within their own interests. The strategy ensured that elites could control the levers of financial and political power among nations to serve their own interests.

The first crude oil gusher was discovered in 1901 in Beaumont, Texas, generating unimaginable wealth for Texaco, Shell, Standard Oil, and Chevron. Two years later, Henry Ford founded Ford Motor Company and produced the first assembly line for automobiles. General Motors followed soon after. As the demand for cars grew, so did the demand for oil and by extension, the profits elites stood to make.

Had America's great industrialists held the highest interests of

United States and its citizens at heart, they would have pursued policy that would have guaranteed the country's energy independence and provided inexpensive, readily available energy to the growing nation and its people. In the process, they could have lifted the working poor into the middle class, ensured the integrity and sovereignty of the United States, and breathed new life into the American dream. As a strong, independent, prosperous, self-sufficient nation, the country could have been a powerful force for good throughout the world, and its people would have flourished. Instead, the oil companies and the elites who controlled them sought to corner energy markets and control the money. By controlling the oil and money supply, elites reasoned, they could control the world.

At the behest of Kissinger, President Richard Nixon created Strategic Energy Reserves in Louisiana and Texas where the United States stockpiled crude oil inventories held in reserve in the event of an energy crisis. Once the prices of oil peaked, those reserves could be tapped, maxing out profits for the oil companies.

Kissinger took pride in his clear-eyed, strategic approach to foreign policy. What he lacked in wisdom and integrity, he possessed in opportunistic cunning and treachery. A Jewish émigré from Germany, he repaid the country that allowed him to achieve the American dream by imposing a devilish nightmare upon its people. Prior to immigrating to the United States, he joined a secret cabal that had financed the Nazis and was secretly trying to subvert the United States from within so that a small, privileged clique could preside over a new world order led by Communist China. Having experienced Nazi Germany firsthand, Kissinger should have known better. Instead he became inebriated with the prospect of the wealth and power he stood to attain by slavishly serving the dark side.

In 1963, while President Lyndon Johnson was waging his "War on Poverty," David Rockefeller sought to create a "managerial task force of free enterprise" to assist developing countries by obligating American taxpayers to finance their infrastructure, thereby freeing up public funds to invest in new markets for corporations overseas and increasing shareholder value. American citizens would not realize significant returns from these investments; yet, they were required to foot the bill through tax increases while the participating corporations shielded their own assets in offshore tax havens and exploited tax loopholes to the fullest extent of the law.

The following year, Rockefeller reach out to retired corporate executives and invited them to join an International Executive Service. Through this program, the globetrotting executives travelled overseas to work with foreign governments to identify problems corporations could solve with American money. Through the IES, Rockefeller-backed corporations secured contracts for hundreds of projects in 45 countries, financed by the Agency for International Development, which was capitalized with public funds.

Rockefeller argued that the taxpayers should invest in free enterprise to promote peace, stability, and prosperity around the world. "A world corporation's very desire for political stability makes it prone to become aligned with governments in power," he said at the time. Instead of stability, the world experienced chaos. Kissinger's strategy of "linkage" ensured that elites could manipulate governments abroad to generate more favorable conditions and profitability for specific Rockefeller and Rothschild aligned corporate interests. In lieu of peace and stability, the world experienced endless wars, enriching elites further through taxpayer supported defense contracts and technology transfers, which compromised U.S. national security, drove up the national debt, and devastated millions of lives. In place of prosperity, Americans experienced deprivation as wealth was redistributed from working people into the hands of the parasitic elites. "Power is the ultimate aphrodisiac," Kissinger once said.

By the time oil was discovered in the Middle East, oil companies were already quite rich. The Arabs had no way of producing their own oil, Williams said.lxiv American and European oil companies were therefore well positioned to divide up the Middle East energy markets among themselves. Among the first American companies to take advantage of the low production costs in the Middle East were Getty, Standard Oil, Continental Oil, and Atlantic Richfield. The "Seven Sisters" dominated the global petroleum industry from the mid 1940s to the mid 1970s. By the time the oil crisis struck in 1973, the Seven Sisters controlled around 85 percent of the world's petroleum.

Oil was discovered at Prudhoe Bay, Alaska in 1966. The oil companies could hardly contain their enthusiasm over the prospect of drilling the Alaskan oil fields. First they had to resolve the issue of land ownership with the Eskimos. Replicating a tried-and-true strategy adopted for the federally recognized Indian tribes in the lower 48 states, a Yale law student by the name of William Van Ness structured the land claimslxv which paid out $962,000,000 to the Alaskan Indians for their land, with 45,000,000 acres of land transferred into regional corporations under the pretext of helping the Natives become economically self sufficient so that they would not have to rely upon the federal government for financial support. As the companies grew profitable, the Indians continued to languish in poverty.

A persistent lobbying effort led by Alaska Sen. Ted Stevens helped resolve the land claims. In 1971, Nixon signed the Alaska Native Claims Settlement Act into law. As the Congressional Record confirms, the oil companies were blocked from developing the fields due to resistance from powerful Native interests, which were secretly controlled by the elites.

By 2009, the Alaska Native Corporations were generating $7,200,000,000 in revenue. Yet the Indians remained poor and continued to demand ever more government money for a myriad of products and services that elites provided in these lucrative, closed, taxpayer supported markets. As the CR reported, "These corporations were formed under the Act to manage the land to create for-profit business ventures."lxvi

While scouting for oil throughout the world, Kissinger embarked on his shuttle diplomacy, fluttering from one country to another like a bat out of hell. If President George Washington, the nation's Founding Father, wisely admonished the United States to avoid foreign entanglements in his Farewell Address, Kissinger, who was knee deep in foreign entanglements, entangled the United States all over the globe, often in areas where it arguably never should been involved in the first place. The result was a hemorrhaging of American blood, treasure, and oil to foreign interests.

The oil companies had secured profitable arrangements with Iran, Saudi Arabia, Iraq, and other Middle Eastern countries. Kissinger had also set his eyes on the Soviet Union, with a view to tapping its Siberian oil fields. "Henry Kissinger traveled to every oil-producing nation in the world," Williams said. If Americans cherished their hard earned independence, Kissinger devilishly played one country against another to leverage the power and influence of the elites. The meddling of the oil companies had disastrous consequences around the world, particularly for the United States, spurring the rise of Islamic terrorism and the demolition of American exceptionalism, with Saudi Arabia emerging as one of the leading sponsors of state terrorism.

Since acquiring petro dollars, the Saudis have poured money into American political campaigns and nonprofits, like the Clinton Foundation,lxvii helping to shape American foreign policy on behalf of a secret cabal. "The Saudi petrodollars that have flooded into the United States during the last 30 years have affected American business, politics, and society," Gerald Posner wrote in <u>Secrets of the Kingdom: The Inside Story of the Saudi-U.S. Connection.</u> "The money had bought the House of Saud a coveted seat at the table with American corporate and political elites, and the Saudis have assiduously courted the access that results from such enormous infusions of cash."

The U.S. oil giants collaborated with foreign governments and geological teams to locate more oil reserves around the world.lxviii After they discovered oil in Iraq in 1927, they anticipated finding oil in Saudi Arabia. Once the Saudis came to power in 1933, they allowed Standard Oil of California broad exploration rights in exchange for financial support for the House of Saud. Standard Oil received an oil concession that covered 360,000 square miles (over 1/3 of Saudi Arabia) for a $35,000 annual fee and two loans totaling $350,000.

The oil companies ignored the religious objections of imams whose opposed foreign meddling within the Kingdom, inspiring Muslim resentment towards the West. Ibn Saud attempted to assuage the concerns of imams and their followers by telling them that it was permissible to use foreigners to "exert to our benefit the metals, oil, and water placed by Allah beneath our land."

The price Standard Oil paid for this benefit was only a fraction of what the rights were actually worth when the company finally struck oil. The reserves were gushers. By some accounts, they were large and capable enough of producing 20 times more than America's best wells at the time.

While being courted by Western oil companies, the Saudi royalty embraced Wahhabi fanaticism, with a view to establishing an Islamic state from Spain to Indonesia, reflecting globalist designs with a radical Muslim face.

Wealth derived from these fields were concentrated within the House of Saud. Lacking financial sophistication, the Saudi royal family engaged in conspicuous consumption, quickly spending itself into financial ruin. The oil companies exploited their financial naiveté to gain leverage within the kingdom. Together they formed a giant consortium called Armaco (Arabian-American Oil Company) that consisted of Standard Oil of California, Texaco, Mobil, and Standard Oil of New Jersey (Exxon), which was granted 60 leases on 400,000 miles of the Saudi peninsula. Oil development was supported by $33,000,000 in U.S. government subsidies, helping Armaco become one of the largest and most profitable corporations in the world.

By the 1980s, Armaco employed over 50,000 people and was generating $50,000,000,000 in revenue, with the House of Saud being the primary beneficiary. With their newfound wealth, the Saudis spread Wahhabism through such organizations as the Muslim World League and offered asylum to the leaders of the Muslim Brotherhood.

In addition to embracing Wahhabi Islam as the only true faith while characterizing Christianity and Judaism as "distorted and twisted religions," the House of Saud acquired influence with the American political establishment, whose unprincipled leaders were quick to adopt the rhetoric of Saudi leaders and champion Saudi interests in exchange for campaign contributions and lucrative contracting opportunities. As the House of Saud gained influence with the West, Christianity came under assault within the United States.

A country once protected by oceans on the east and west and friendly neighbors to the north and south would eventually experience terrorism within its own borders brought on by misguided policies within the Middle East. Osama bin Laden, a Saudi citizen who assumed credit for the terrorist attacks against the World Trade Center and Pentagon on September 11, 2001, was linked to a fund with the Carlyle Group that invested in buyouts of military and aerospace companies, representing Muslim anger towards the West.lxix

In the face of Western meddling in the Middle East and Arab resentment over America's close relationship with Israel, the House of Saud tried to counter what it perceived to be America's "incredibly effective American Jewish lobby" with a lobby of its own, leading Saudis to pour money into the American political system to sway U.S. foreign policy, shape public opinion, and secure public funds for its own interests, which aligned with those of the cabal.lxx After presiding over the World Bank and Chase Manhattan Bank, for example, John McCloy was retained as lobbyist for Armaco to hand deliver a letter from the Chairmen of Exxon, Mobil, Texaco, and

Standard Oil to Nixon, recommending that he limit his support of Israel on grounds that the Jewish state was the source of all the instability in the Middle East. The House of Saud, which was deeply suspicious of Israel, attempted to warn the United States that Israel was secretly controlled by Russian communists.

As part of a strategy to inspire Saudi trust, Armaco's executives paid lip service to opposing Israel. Armaco also successfully lobbied the Treasury Department to treat royalty payments to the Saudis as taxes, thereby reducing its federal tax liability from $50,000,000 to $6,000,000. CIA agents were even recruited to join Armaco's PR and Government Relations team to influence American policy.lxxi Upon discovering that the Saudis were fond of young boys, the CIA procured them for the royal family; the company even lobbied for exemption from New York's anti-discrimination laws in 1959 so that it could force applicants to disclose their religious affiliation to avoid offending the Saudis by accidentally hiring a Jew.

After building up the security and defense of the Saudis, the Nixon Administration began transferring America's technology to Israel through such organizations as the U.S.-Israeli Bi-National Science Foundation, which was founded in 1972 to promote scientific relations between the two countries through collaborative research projects. The group was established in Israel to avoid U.S. oversight and keep Americans in the dark. While helping Arab countries extract oil, Kissinger promoted the 1975 Memorandum of Understanding, which guaranteed Israel's oil needs in the event of a future crisis; at the same time, Kissinger prevented the United States from tapping its own reserves in Alaska, rendering the United States vulnerable to political upheavals within the Middle East that elites were fomenting by playing both sides against the middle. In turn, the United States was reduced to a patsy who subsidized foreign countries and sustained the losses for foreign meddling.

After Kissinger opened up channels for transferring U.S. technology to Israel, Israel proceeded to pass that technology on to Communist China. Amir Bohot and Yaakov Katz's book, <u>The Weapon Wizards: How Israel Became a High-Tech Military Superpower</u>, reveals how a delegation of high ranking Israelis traveled to meet with a Chinese delegation in 1979. "Until that winter day," the authors wrote, "Israeli defense officials had never been to China. The two countries did not have diplomatic ties, and nobody on the Israeli side—except for the members of the delegation, the prime minister, the defense minister, and a handful of others—knew about the trip. If word got out, Israel knew that the Americans would be furious."

By 1979, the IDF Talpiot program was launched to support an Israeli-Chinese relationship, which helped transfer U.S. technology to China vis-à-vis Israel, establishing the basis for what would later become the Belt and Road Initiative, helping China emerge as a credible threat to the United States economically, strategically, and militarily. The cabal had planned this outcome at the end of World War II. Israel and China's treacherous leaders were just as complicit as America's, having sold out their own people and national interests in a quest for wealth, power, and status conferred through admission into powerful, parasitic cabal.

Kissinger's philosophy of linkages also applied to people. The more people could be compromised and dependent upon the elite structure, the less likely dissenters were to act independently to challenge them. The elites therefore nurtured dependency among the people and among leaders to consolidate their own control.

Israel, whose origins trace to the Rothschilds and the Balfour Declaration, was merely serving as a proxy agent for the elites. Speaking presciently, Ben Gurion, the first Prime Minister of Israel, announced in 1930 that he was a Bolshevik and that Israeli citizens viewed the USSR as "our homeland."[lxxii] As the Israeli newspaper, *Haaretz* reported, "Many of this country's early inhabitants were Russian-born. They spoke Russian, read books and sang songs in Russian, and thought and dreamed in Russian. Many of them owed their lives to the Red Army's war against Nazi Germany. Stalin was considered the father of the victory over Hitler."

The Soviet Union was at the center of the Israeli identity, Ben Gurion said, conceding that China is "weak, but a great world power in the future." As will later be revealed, the Yalta conference, where the British, American, and Russian leaders negotiated the terms for world peace, made allowances for the rise of China.

In the Middle East, elites were playing both sides against the middle. Chase Manhattan Bank, for example, served as trustee of an Israeli bond issue while encouraging Nixon to strengthen U.S. financial relationships with the Arabs. As its Chair, David Rockefeller said, "in international banking, you often get involved in this way."lxxiii

By the time Ibn Saud died in 1952, he had frittered away $400,000,000 of the country's oil revenue on himself and his family, investing little in the country's infrastructure and defense. At the same time, Israel was emerging as a threat to its interests. The elites confounded matters further by transferring U.S. technology to Saudi Arabia, which was exporting Wahhabi terrorism through the world and arming al Qaeda terrorists. Terrorists were then weaponized against the West, providing a pretext for the erosion of civil liberties in the United States in order to neutralize the new Islamic threat.

Elite meddling in the Middle East further stoked resentment among the Muslim populations who opposed what they perceived to be Western attempts to corrupt and control their leaders and countries. Saudi Arabia kept one sandal in the world of radical Islam and another in the West while exporting Wahhabism throughout the world through radicals armed with technology and weaponry provided and funded by the U.S. government.

The Saudis were largely compliant to the demands of Western oil companies until Libyan dictator Muammar Gaddafi broke rank and demanded higher royalty payments from American oil firms. Faced with the rise of nationalism, the oil companies quickly made concessions to Libya, emboldening other oil Middle Eastern countries to demand higher payments for their oil as well. By 1972, the major oil companies had formed a cartel, the Organization of Petroleum Exporting Countries (OPEC), to gain leverage against Western oil companies who were attempting to form their own cartel within Indian Country. By 1972, Western oil companies conceded to OPEC's demands and agreed to more favorable terms in which to extract oil from Arab lands.

While Qaddafi won a small victory, standing up for Libyan interests placed a target on his back. Not only had he challenged the oil consortium, but he refused to decouple the Libyan currency from the gold standard, preventing elites from being able to manipulate its currency and indebt the country. As Secretary of State, Kissinger's protégé, Hillary Clinton, would take care of Qaddafi. "We came, he saw, he died," she giddily clapped and laughed, alluding to Roman Emperor Julius Caesar memorable words as she celebrated Quaddafi's quick death through a NATO airstrike on Libya.

Kissinger used the Saudis' dependency on oil revenue to help the cabal gain leverage there while weakening the United States. "The Saudi Arabians were nomads on camels," Pastor Lindsey Williams said. "Kissinger offered to make them rich, to cut them a deal. He said, 'If you go along, we'll buy oil from you in America.' He made the Arab sheikhs denominate all oil sales in dollars so that they could use a percentage of their money to build infrastructure, all supplied by U.S. corporations, and use some of the money to buy the American debt."

The Saudis readily agreed to Kissinger's terms. While America's debt was backed with the surety of the American government, the Saudis did not know that the Federal Reserve was not part of the government itself nor did they know that the United States was creating debt to support Big Business while weakening its own economic position.

One of the most in-demand commodities in the world was oil whose price is denominated in dollars. Yet, as Williams said, the price of oil and most of the profits generated through oil production were not set by the oil companies or oil producing nations but by the World Bank, which had tapped U.S. taxpayers to extend loans to third world countries to expand markets for transnational corporations. Once those countries defaulted on the loans, the World Bank was positioned to seize valuable assets held as collateral. After Nixon removed the dollar from the gold standard, the Saudis were told to purchase oil in dollars. In return, the Saudis received American taxpayer supported protection against their enemies. The rest of the world was forced to hold a high amount of dollars in their reserves to purchase U.S. debt, placing the dollar at the center of the global financial and economic system. The petro dollar was born.

According to the Strategic Culture Foundation, an online platform that provides commentary on Eurasian and global affairs,lxxiv "As long as the U.S. continues to maintain its dominance of the global financial and economic system, thanks to the dollar, its supremacy as a world superpower is hardly questioned. To maintain this influence on the currency markets..., the pricing of oil in U.S. dollars is crucial....The relationship has been mutually beneficial. The House of Saud has been free to run its own country according to the strictures of Wahhabism without Western interference, and Washington enjoys a capacity for unlimited military spending especially after the 2008 crisis and the beginning of quantitative easing simply through the printing of debt in the form of bonds that are immediately acquired by other countries....Washington has effectively been printing waste paper and obtaining consumer goods in return, a state of affairs that has allowed the United States to squander six trillion dollars in wars in Iraq and Afghanistan without suffering significant economic consequences."

After the Second World War, the elites set about to shore up more markets for their corporations through public-funded infrastructure development and entitlement programs. The more government was enlisted to provide for its citizens, as opposed to empowering them to provide for themselves, the more public funds could be allocated to the private sector, thereby enabling elites to acquire wealth through public-private partnerships and government contracts. Among the greatest tools to secure control over a country and its people was debt.

In the interests of alleviating poverty, the World Bank siphoned funds from the relatively wealthy Western nations and their middle classes to extend loans to third world countries to build their infrastructure and provide services for their poor, all in the name of global sustainability and compassion. Politically connected corporations were then contracted for the work. In order to secure the loan, the desperate country targeted in the scopes of the elites was required to provide collateral, which would take the form of a valuable asset. The conditions of the loans were quite stringent, often guaranteeing default. Upon default, the World Bank would take possession of the asset.lxxv In the process, the corporations would profit through controlled, taxpayer supported and government facilitated markets, the World Bank and the elites would acquire the assets from the targeted country, and the country which acquired the loan to better itself would fall into debt, allowing international bankers leverage over it. Global business was being financed by the productive middle class who were rapidly losing their standing to subsidize the lavish lifestyles of elites through government contracts and rising taxes.

The global financial system was not created to alleviate poverty, but to spread it around. Its process of lending and debt amounted to a global redistribution of wealth and economic leveling, with elites concocting ever more strategies to shore up the world's wealth and power into their own hands while the rest of the world descended into poverty and helplessness. God created a world of abundance, with mankind assigned the task of wise stewardship over its resources. Yet wise stewardship necessarily requires a noble leadership, and the elites were ignoble at best. While the corrupt royals of the old world pranced around like effete aristocrats, drinking the finest wines, eating the richest foods, and engaging in the most decadent lifestyles in the most opulent homes on the choicest parcels of land, the surrounding peasants were relegated to a life of misery and despair. If life for the people was like a box of chocolates, for elites, it was a Game of Thrones. They would be tragic, pitiful figures if the devastation their greed and foolishness inflicted upon the rest of the world weren't so profound.

Furthering elite schemes were the aptly named Bank of Reconstruction and Development and its sister organization, the International Monetary Fund, which were created in 1944 at the Bretton Woods Conference after World War II. The Bank of Reconstruction and Development was soon renamed the World Bank. Within a few years, the World Bank was providing $447,000,000 in loans backed by taxpayers. By 2015, the World Bank was granting more than $60,000,000,000 in loans per year, generating contracting opportunities for the parasitic elites who never seemed to lose their appetite for the public's money.

In 1969, the IMF created an international reserve asset called the Special Drawing Rights to transact trade in a single currency. The SDR consisted of the American dollar, European euro, the Japanese yen, and the British pound. Together, they were called a basket of currencies, as Hillary Clinton, the face of globalism, knew all too well. One month before the 2016 presidential election which Hillary expected to win, the Chinese reminibi was added to the basket, with elites privately planning to trade oil in reminibi with a view to having Communist China lead the new world order. On the campaign trail, Hillary disparaged the supporters of her nationalist rival, Donald Trump, as a "basket of deplorables." The pun-prone Hillary had in this moment tipped her hand to reveal the elite agenda as she alluded to those who rejected globalism and its basket of currencies as racists, sexists, homophobes, Islamophobes, basically dismissing American citizens as knuckle dragging Neanderthals. All that stood in the way of the China-led new world order was Donald Trump.

The system was being rigged, Pastor Lindsey Williams said. Just look at the conflicts of interest surrounding President Barack

Obama's Secretary of Treasury, Tim Geithner, he observed. No major corporation would have allowed executives to serve on the Boards of competitors, given conflicts of interest, he said. Yet, while Geithner was Chairman of the Federal Reserve, he presided over the Bank of International Settlements. Geithner, whose father had worked for Ford Motor Company and assisted Rockefeller's political campaigns, was affiliated with the International Monetary Fund and Kissinger Associates, reflecting his allegiance to the cabal. "Not only did he preside over the U.S. Central Bank," Williams said. "But he is Director of the (BIS)," which is the Central Bank for the 60 Central Banks which foster international and monetary cooperation throughout the globe. How did Geithner rigorously champion national and global interests at the same time? He didn't. Rather, he betrayed national interests on behalf of globalists. As Treasury Secretary, for example, he presided over a $700,000,000,000 bailout for Wall Street, essentially allowing elites to create the conditions upon which to crash the economy, causing many working, law abiding Americans to lose their jobs, homes, pensions, and assets while rewarding elites with taxpayer bailouts for the trouble.

    The BIS had originally facilitated Germany's reparations after the World Wars. As part of that deal, the German people were forced to pay $23,000,000 to the corporations for machinery and manufacturing. Not only had the corporations profited from Hitler's rise, but they profited again through his demise. Through the OSS, Nazi scientists were recruited into the international intelligence networks and allowed to immigrate to the United States to develop new technologies. The result was a psychopathic technocratic class who sought to control the world, its resources, and its wealth through any means necessary. The globalists then set their sights on the United States.

    "Unless something is done, America will be a has been," Williams said. "They are trying to bankrupt the United States so that they can scoop up the nation's assets on pennies on the dollar after the nation has been thoroughly bankrupted. They have diminished our lifestyles to raise theirs, reducing us to the level of third world countries. They make us pay for our own demise at the gas pump. The one thing that touches the lives of everything is oil, their method for controlling the world."

    After World War II, the elites destabilized the Middle East to control that region's wealth and oil. When the Arab-Israeli war broke out in 1973, the Arabs organized OPEC to oppose the federal government's decision to help the Israeli military gain leverage in post-war peace negotiations. The subsequent 1973 oil embargo strained the U.S. economy, and yet, Williams said, the United States need not have been affected at all as it had more than enough oil in Alaska to meet its energy demands for hundreds of years. Yet, the Nixon Administration refused to allow the oil companies to touch those fields.

As Secretary of State, Henry Kissinger proceeded to weaken the United States through debt and interdependence. By enlisting foreign governments to buy U.S. debt, Kissinger ensured that the United States could put up the money for an unlimited number of government contracts, both foreign and domestic. Foreign countries would purchase that debt by virtue of the surety of government bonds and the good reputation of the United States. As a result, the American taxpayers were left on the hook to finance the development of infrastructure around the world, leading to the creation of impressive cities and establishments overseas that make the United States look like a third world country by comparison. It also enabled the United States to squander money on wars in Iraq and Afghanistan, generating profits for corporations while shoring up Iraq's oil for Israel. The corporations that secured the contracts reaped the financial rewards while American citizens were burdened with the debt. It would not be long before their jobs would be shipped overseas too as these corporations sought cheap labor and reduced regulatory standards to enhance their balance sheets even further.

Kissinger convinced the Saudis to purchase U.S. Treasury notes from oil proceeds so that they could invest in their own infrastructure development, technology, and defense. In the process, he generated even more opportunities for multinationals. By 1979, the Saudis had invested $27,000,000,000 in U.S. contracts and $30,000,000,000 in U.S. real estate, government security, and stock options. Eventually they acquired interests in News Corp., Apple, Yahoo, TWA, Hewlett Packard, eBay, Amazon, Microsoft, Planet Hollywood, and Microsoft, companies that had become rich through globalism. General Motors, which has received numerous U.S. taxpayer-funded bail outs, established Saudi Arabia Motors Company on the Saudi peninsula.lxxvi In 2004, Prince Al-Waleed reportedly engaged Hank Greenberg to discuss opportunities for AIG to expand into Saudi Arabia. Is it any wonder American's leading corporations prefer globalism to nationalism?

"The (Saudi) government is spending enormous sums to build the necessary physical infrastructure to create the modern administrative structure needed both to regulate and encourage manufacturing," a spokesman for the Jeddah Chamber of Commerce said. "We have a growing body of skilled workers, widespread consumer prosperity, increased contracts with the outside world, and an entirely new breed of industrialists."lxxvii This result was achieved on the backs of American taxpayers, who have shouldered the financial burden, enabling the Saudis to create a thriving middle class while U.S. infrastructure crumbles and its own middle class struggles to get by.

As the world's largest oil exporter, Saudi Arabia plowed $300,000,000 into an International Airport in Jeddah, an estimated $340,000,000 for a 400 mile Talif-Abha-Tizan highway, and $55,000,000 for telecommunications projects to name a few of its splurges. These projects came about with support from the Ford Foundation, UN agencies, and private consulting firms through a National Development Plan supported by economists from the Stanford Research Institute, which has advised the U.S. Air Force, Chevron, and Walt Disney and worked with venture capital firms that launched Apple's SIRI, Salesforces Tempo AI, and Google's Redwood Robotics. Tech companies have benefited from access to global markets, supported by American taxpayers only to engage in aggressive public relations and lobbying efforts to disparage the very Americans who made their success possible. These companies have supported the H1-BI visa program that has provided hiring preferences for immigrants over American citizens, with Disney generating headlines after American employees were told to train their less expensive foreign replacements.lxxviii

President Dwight Eisenhower warned the American people about the Military Industrial Complex that was weakening the United States economically and militarily, to which Armaco executives responded: "To the new international corporations, any nation which threatens freedom of trade and communications... is as welcome as a kick in the head. ...Ever since Eisenhower issued the famous warning.., it has been open season on corporations – dark suspicious that capitalism and militarism are intrinsically linked.... Managers belong to a world community, not national communities....They are 'men without a country' in the sense that we are not beholden to one nation and do not owe allegations to one government....Banks are crossing national boundaries (and have formed) teams which, more likely than not, involve institutions from other nations, often nations that are not particularly friendly in a political sense....The average American is unaware that Unilever, Shell, Nestle....and other business are (now) owned by foreign capital."

***

As the elites set their sights on the Middle East, Iran and Iraq attempted to exert their independence. As a consequence, they were targeted for regime change. Iran's first democratically elected Prime Minister, Mohammed Mosaddegh, was toppled in a coup organized by the CIA and M-I5 after he attempted to nationalized the Iranian oil industry which the British had previously controlled. "Our long years of negotiations with foreign countries… have yielded no results," Mosaddegh told the International Court of Justice. "With the oil revenues, we could meet our entire budget and combat poverty, disease, and backwardness among our people." While defending himself against charges of treason, the ousted Iranian leader conceded that the damage inflicted upon Iran through a "system of political and economic exploitation by the world's greatest empires" had been built upon what he called "a savage and dreadful system of international espionage and colonialism."

After Mosaddegh was overthrown, he was replaced with a hand-picked, pro-Western Shah, who invited the foreign oil companies to return to Iran. The Consortium of Iran consisted of BP, Gulf Oil, Royal Dutch Shell, and four Armaco partners, including Standard Oil of California (Chevron), Standard Oil of New Jersey (Exxon), Standard Oil of New York (Mobil), and Texaco, forming the Seven Sisters. The coup against the popular leader spurred nationalist opposition to the Shah-backed Western oil companies. Try as they might, the oil companies could not recover their position in Iran. The Shah was subsequently deposed in the 1979 Revolution, paving the way for the emergence of a radical Islamic republic under the Ayatollah Khomeini.

In 1991, President George H.W. Bush took aim at Iraq. Needing a pretext for war, the United States government reportedly supplied Kuwait with enough drills to steal 300,000 barrels of oil from Iraq per day. The theft was valued at $3,000,000,000 annually, enabling Kuwait to flood the market with oil to drive down prices. Bush encouraged the Iraqi leader, Saddam Hussein, to invade Kuwait to protect its reserves, advising that the United States had no interest in the matter. Once Iraq took the bait, Bush declared war to "liberate Kuwait," citing satellite images of Iraqi troops threatening U.S. oil supplies. Bush's pretext for war crumbled under the light of scrutiny after investigative journalists from the *St. Petersburg Times* acquired images that revealed that the area in question was just empty desert. Bush subsequently lost re-election to Bill Clinton, a fellow globalist.

A decade later, President George W. Bush finished the job his father had started. Just like his father, he concocted a lie as a pretext for war. In an effort to justify attacking Iraq after al Qaeda terrorists struck the World Trade Center and Pentagon on September 11, 2001, the younger Bush declared that Saddam Hussein was harboring terrorists and weapons of mass destruction.

The ensuing Operation Iraqi Freedom resulted in the deaths of hundreds of thousands of people and drained the U.S. Treasury of billions of dollars, with lucrative contracts doled out to the Alaska Native Corporations. "Those weapons of mass destruction got to be somewhere," the younger Bush joked at a National Correspondents dinner. "Nope, no weapons over there. Maybe under here!"

To observers, the elites appeared completely indifferent to the human suffering their wars had caused. Misguided policies in the Middle East had brought terrorism to America's door. In order to protect Americans, U.S. citizens were required to surrender their civil liberties and endure personal indignities as elites expanded the surveillance state, generating billions of dollars in defense contracts for themselves.

With American power in decline, China agreed to buy Russia's oil with a view to denominating oil in the Chinese renmibi, Williams said. The goal was to usurp the United States as world leader. Elites salivated over the vast, untapped markets in China with its 1,500,000,000 people who could supply virtually unlimited cheap labor and consumers for their government-supported goods and services. Infected with corrupt elites, the United States was arming and financing the rise of Israel, Russia, and China.

"There is no such thing, as Soviet technology," Stanford

researcher Anthony Sutton told the Platform Committee of the Republican Party in the 1980s. "Almost all – perhaps 90-95 percent – came directly or indirectly from the United States and its allies. In effect, the United States and the NATO countries have built the Soviet Union, its industrial and military capabilities. The massive construction job has taken 50 years. Since the Revolution of 1917, it has been carried out through trade and sale of plant equipment, and technical assistance, military technology transfers up to the 1980s."

Vice President Dick Cheney once boasted that "deficits don't matter." The deficit didn't matter, Williams said, as the United States was simply obligated to pay the interest on the debt. The Chinese had purchased trillions of dollars in U.S. debt on a fool's mission, he said. At the end of the day, they were just buying paper, which was no longer backed by gold.

A transnational shadow elite was wrecking havoc on the global economy, with former Goldman Sachs Managing Director Nomi Prins observing that[lxxix] "major central banks predominantly of the developed world and in particular, the G-3, Federal Reserve, European Central Bank, and Bank of Japan have colluded to produce an exorbitant amount of capital through their own mechanisms in a way that was unlimited, in a way that was unregulated, in a way that is not particularly transparent by way of where the money went except in the asset bubbles it has produced. There is $14,500,000,000,000 worth of artificial, electronically conjured, money induced by just these three central banks. Then throw in the Peoples Bank of China, which uses it for different purposes and you're up $22,000,000,000,000 worth of subsidies for the financial system and markets....Once that's leveraged through corporations, governments and countries borrow because rates have been so cheap in the developed world during this period. They create a record amount of debt. And now we have a situation of $22,000,000,000,000 in subsidies that weren't there 10 years ago. We now have a record amount of debt. We have a perspective from emerging markets that currencies are devalued more than normal relative to the dollar in the wake of this, resulting in inequality throughout the world, financial uncertainty, financial bubbles...If you dumped $22,000,000,000,000 of debt onto the market you would create an absolute collapse.... The world wouldn't can't exist on debt."

***

While elites were traipsing around the globe tapping overseas oil markets, the Council of Energy Resource Tribes was tapping energy in Indian Country. Launched in 1975 and funded by the Nixon Administration, CERT was established by Navajo Nation Chairman Peter McDonald, who was under the advisement of Ahmed Kooros, the Vice President of Economic Affairs for the Central Bank of Iran and Minister of Oil and Development of Iran, who represented OPEC and the Shah of Iran in meetings. A number of oil companies were involved in the creation of CERT including ARCO, Exxon, Gulf Oil, and others. While advising CERT, Kooros negotiated a right-of-way contract between the Navajos and Atlantic Richfield Company, with the Navajos attempting to form a "Navajo League of Nations," modeled after the League of Nations, to pursue a "convergence of Indian policy with the national consensus on major national energy policy goals."[lxxx]

While the Navajos were cashing in on energy, the General Accounting Office uncovered a housing kickback scheme in which $13,300,000 earmarked for the Navajo Housing Authority had been redirected into private hands.

Today CERT reportedly controls five percent of the nation's oil, 10 percent of gas, 30 percent of the coal, 30 percent of the low sulfur coral reserves, and 40 percent of the nation's mineable uranium. These numbers don't even begin to take into account renewable energy sources like solar, wind, and geothermal resources -- tribal energy reserves worth upwards of billions of dollars.

Some researchers claim that over $100,000,000,000 in oil remains to be recovered on Indian lands through fracking. CERT has affirmed publicly that it aspires to secure "the energy future for all Americans" while demanding that tribes, and by extension, their controllers, "have absolute control of their own resources."

One member of the Cheyenne River Sioux Tribe joined the Army Corps of Engineers to contract with the Rio Tinto Group, a British multinational and mining corporation headquartered in London which is linked to the Rothschilds. Rio Tinto's rise follows the typical monopolistic pattern of the nation's leading industrialists. In 1968, Rio Tinto acquired U.S. Borax, which controls the world's largest deposits of the industrial mineral. In 1989, Rio Tinto bought British Petroleum's failing mining unit for $4,300,000,000. In 2000, Rio

Tinto acquired major aluminum, iron ore, diamond, and coal assets for $4,000,000. Most recently, Rio Tinto has made inroads into China.

Another Navajo tribal member , Steve Grey, worked for the Department of Energy's Lawrence Livermore National Lab's American Indian Program, where scientists allegedly doctored their own research and technology to create a climate a fear in order to generate sales, Michael Crichton, the author of <u>Jurrassic Park </u>and <u>State of Fear.</u> claimed.

Many of the energy-rich tribes have become fabulously wealthy through casinos and government contracting while the taxpayers have subsidized them. The tribes are generating enough wealth to be self-sustaining, and yet they continue to approach the federal government with tin cup in hand. "When the Navajo Nation gets to a million population, the taxpayers, they're not going to afford us," a Navajo Indian said.lxxxi "They're having a hard time right now. They're the government. They're the one that's giving us money to live. They cannot afford us no more with more Native American population growth. They're saying right now at the Hill, you go to the Hill, this is what I hear: 'Man, I can't even afford my own kids. I can't even take them to college anymore, and yet my tax is going out.' They complain about the war. They complain about the fuel costs. They complain about us. 'When are these Native Americans going to get on their feet? We've been putting money all my life in there. Still today, we're still putting money in it.' It's talk out there right now. Believe it."

Through the tribes, the elites were slowly introducing European social democracy into the United States. Founding Father George Washington was right to warn the country about foreign entanglements. Two centuries after the American Revolution, foreign interests had insinuated themselves throughout American society, creating all sorts of problems that need never have occurred had the nation remained true to its founding principles – and vigilant. The Indian tribes were testament to this.

And then there was Kissinger.

***

Kissinger's career traces to the occupation and reconstruction of Nazi Germany. "The military defeat of the Nazi regime and the post-war presence of American forces in Europe transformed Kissinger from a refugee into a ruler," the *Executive Intelligence Review* reported.lxxxii The future Secretary of State was recruited by William "Wild Bill" Donovan to gather intelligence during World War II. He was placed with the U.S. Army and assigned to work on intelligence and counter-intelligence to apprehend Nazis and gather information on the advanced technology they had been secretly developinglxxxiii "This was not an accidental assignment," The *EIR* reported. "William Donovan, the head of the OSS, pressured the Army and other American military institutions to promote German Jewish émigrés."

While working in intelligence, Kissinger became connected to the Round Table, a group established by agents of the British Crown and affiliated business interests who were seeking to exploit "economic resources and political power to advance British finance capital."lxxxiv Among its distinguished members were Viscount Astor and Arthur Balfour, who authored the Balfour Declaration during World War I that promised Palestine to Lord Rothschild as a home for the Jewish people. The group became "the centre of the aristocratic power bloc that has dominated the British government throughout the (last) century."lxxxv

The aristocrats' greatest prize was China. As a young man, Kissinger was mentored by UK Prime Minister Lord Alec Douglas-Home,lxxxvi who advocated opening China to the West. Among Douglas-Home's esteemed colleagues were Lord Bertrand Russell, a socialist philosopher whose students included Mao Tse-tung and (future Chinese Premier) Chou En Lai – Chinese leaders whom Kissinger would engage across the diplomatic table as Secretary of State while serving "powers dedicated to the weakening of the United States (as) an avowed agent of British oligarchic interests."lxxxvii

After immigrating to the United States, Kissinger joined the Council of Foreign Relations, where he was taken under the wing of David and Nelson Rockefeller who tapped him to serve on the CFR Board of Directors and on the Editorial Board of *Foreign Affairs*, the organization's foreign policy journal. The CFR has since endowed a Henry H. Kissinger Chair in U.S. Foreign Policy, reflecting Kissinger's passionate and effective dedication to the Rockefellers' global designs.

Harboring political ambitions of his own, Richard Nixon aligned himself with the Rockefeller Republicans as a presidential candidate and then proceeded to normalize relations with China as

President.

While the global elite were keen to open China's markets, China was interested in curtailing Soviet imperialism. Nixon began transferring U.S. technology to China for this purpose. As Stanford University researcher Anthony Sutton warned in 1984, "Communist China will be a superpower built by American technology and skill" within 15 years.[lxxxviii]

Nixon's Liaison Office in Beijing was led by David Bruce, an OSS agent whom Averell Harriman described as "the most brilliant representative of our country abroad in my generation."[lxxxix] Bruce, who had worked for Harriman's international banking firm, had attempted to acquire the *Washington Post* at a bankruptcy sale only to lose out to Eugene Mayer, who became First President of the World Bank and Chairman of the Federal Reserve. After the war, Bruce followed Harriman into the Commerce Department. While coordinating the Marshall Plan, Harriman forged a close relationship with Jean Monnet, the architect of the European Coal and Steel Community, a precursor to a European common market envisioned by the Rothschilds.

Conceding that the CIA "can't do anything that (the Chinese) won't know anyway," Kissinger reminded Bruce that his effectiveness "depended on the Chinese understanding from the beginning that (you are) the President's man – (Mao) wants CIA technicians running the U.S. Office Communications System."[xc] As Secretary of State, Kissinger was granted "unprecedented authority over the national security policy making apparatus, the Kissinger Transcripts reveal. During Kissinger's tenure, the British Crown was allowed to issue National Security Memorandum to federal agencies, including the State Department, Defense Department, CIA, Arms Control and Disarmament Agency (ACDA) to prepare Special Studies to determine where policy changes needed to be made.

Kissinger was known for "having a penchant for back channel communications with foreign governments while keeping the State Department in the dark."[xci] The Secretary of State famously wanted to know what one person he could call to coordinate policy with all the myriad European countries which individually held divergent views and competing interests in a somewhat sardonic swipe at nationalism.

He told Mao, "It is very important that you and we understand what we are going to do and to coordinate our actions."

His objective, transcripts reveal, was to claim executive authority to lower barriers to trade without Congressional approval.

Amb. Huang Hua, a Communist Party revolutionary who headed the People's Republic of China's UN mission and helped normalize relations between the two countries, was one of Kissinger's back channels. Huang and Kissinger held secret meetings at the CIA safe house in the Lower East Side of Manhattan.

At the time, the Secretary of State boasting that George H.W. Bush "is the only person outside the White House who knows I come here."[xcii]

While Kissinger was Secretary of State, David Rockefeller, as Chairman of Chase Manhattan Bank, met with the Chinese Premier to pursue strategies to open up markets in Communist China for Western corporations so that he could link them into global scientific networks.

"My colleagues in Washington think I'm a raving maniac," Kissinger said.[xciii]

"Fundamental cooperation is needed," Mao reminded him.

"Even if we sometimes criticize each other, we will coordinate our actions with you," Kissinger told Mao. "Both of us must be true to our principles....In fact, it would confuse the issue if we spoke the same language....A strong and independent China (is) clearly in our interests and in the interests of world peace."

"I like rightists," Mao said. "That is the Republican Party...I am comparatively happy when people on the right come into power."[xciv]

The difference between the political right and political left are that "those on the right can do what those on the left only talk about," Nixon said.

"There is another point - those of the left are pro-Soviet and would not encourage a move towards the People's Republic," Kissinger said. "We thought all socialist/communist states were the same phenomenon."

"The whole world should unite to defeat...all reactionaries and establish socialism," Mao replied.

To leverage China's power, Kissinger sought to "enmesh" the Soviets in a framework of political obligation and economic dependency that would paralyze them.[xcv]

While he was selling U.S. technology to the USSR, Kissinger was telling the Chinese that "the prospect of U.S. technology (will) moderate their foreign policy conduct through a strategy of keeping the Soviets dependent."

Mao and Kissinger also discussed a strategy of changing U.S. immigration policy to weaken the United States from within.

"Do you want our Chinese women," Mao asked with deadpanned seriousness. "We can give you 10,000,000. We can let them flood your country with disaster and therefore impair your interests."

Kissinger complimented Mao's "novel idea" and advised, "I will have to study it."

"You can set up a committee," Mao suggested. "That is how you settle the population question."

Around this time, Sen. Ted Kennedy, who nursed political ambitions of his own, took steps to permanently change America's immigration policies, with a view toward transforming the country's demographics forever.

"You can let in so many nationalities," Mao said.

While observing his Chinese counterpart, Kissinger perceived a "mocking, slightly demonic smile."[xcvi]

While the globalists were fond of accusing Americans of racism, Kissinger privately acknowledged their tolerance. "There is no feeling of hostility at all toward the Chinese people," he told Mao. "On the contrary, between us right now, there is only a judicial problem, which we will solve in the next years...there is a strong community of interests which is operating immediately....on relations with other countries that have intentions."

Mao laughed with Kissinger over his view of the United States as a "paper tiger," referencing a powerful, but ultimately ineffectual force that could fold with a gust of wind.

Israeli Prime Minister Bibi Netanyahu, who is pursuing commercial opportunities within Chinese markets on behalf of Israel, has reportedly expressed similar sentiments. "Once we squeeze all we can out of the United States, it can dry up and blow away," he said.[xcvii]

As transcripts revealed, Vice Premier Deng Xiaoping praised Kissinger for "(pulling) the wool over the eyes of the West, (demoralizing) the Western people, and (letting) them slacken their pace."

Kissinger's assistant, Winston Lord, who had joined the National Security Council in 1969 went on to become Ambassador to

China during the Bush and Reagan Administrations. President Bill Clinton then appointed Lord Undersecretary of State for East Asia and Pacific Affairs, ensuring that the agenda continued regardless of whom the people elected to serve them. The good, decent, and trusting American people were largely oblivious to the machinations at play as the shadow dragon gradually executed a plan against them which was conceived nearly a century earlier among a small group of men in London.

V.
Treacherous Politicians

The United States is the only country in the world that was created of, by, and for the people. Its founders fled the tyranny, corruption, and oppression of the old world to create a new world, one whose elected representatives served the people, not the powerful. Cognizant of old world treachery, having experienced it first hand, the nation's founders risked their lives to keep foreign interests at bay and establish a government that curtailed abuses of power. With an enduring belief in God, they righteously believed that a noble people did not need an oppressive, expansive government as they could effectively regulate themselves. The government need only intervene when the rights of one infringed upon the rights of another. As Christians, they believed in free will. They elected leaders drawn from their communities who represented their interests. Their rulers were, in effect, public servants – that is, servants of the people.

The people who established the United States were a determined, self-reliant lot who did not rely upon government handouts for their survival. They provided for themselves, helped others as needed, lived within the golden mean, and adhered to a faith which compelled them to be frugal, industrious, and charitable to others. Business was conducted with integrity, often on a handshake. These were the people who made the American dream possible and established a prosperous, well functioning, stable society that became the envy of the world.

The British Empire never got over the loss of their American colony. During the American Revolution, the well trained British militia was handily defeated by colonists who were as resourceful and determined as the British were regimented.

In 1891, a secret meeting was held in London to map out a strategy for "the expansion of British rule throughout the world ...and the ultimate recovery of the United States as an integral part of the British empire." The organization was modeled after the Jesuits, whose intrigue and secrecy had amassed tremendous wealth and power for the Vatican. Among its participants was Cecil Rhodes, a Rothschild-backed agent who amassed a fortune mining diamonds in South Africa. As the *New York Times* reported in 1902, Rhodes believed that "a wealthy secret society should work to secure the world's peace and a British-American Federation."xcviii In 1902, Lord Rothschild affirmed that it would be a good thing if the United States were to return to the British Empire, with Rhodes suggesting that "the only thing feasible to carry out our idea is a secret society gradually absorbing the wealth of the world."xcix The Pilgrim Society and international banks, including Goldman Sachs and JP Morgan, were among the supporters of the plan.

Gradually and through stealth, the world's resources and wealth were swept upwards into the hands of parasitic, degenerate elites who aspired to lord themselves over everyone else. With Rothschild as his advisor, Rhodes mapped out his Last Will and Testament. creating a Rhodes Scholarship that offered promising postgraduate students an opportunity to study at the University of Oxford with the view to acquiring the skills, contacts, and leadership ability needed to drive unity among the English Speaking Union – that is, to carry out the agenda of the secret society for a one world government. Among the recipients of the coveted Rhodes Scholarship was Bill Clinton, a charismatic young man from Arkansas. The Yale-educated Governor of Arkansas, Winthrop Rockefeller, perceived great promise in Bill and his desperately ambitious wife, Hillary, and decided to mentor the ethically challenged, hopelessly greedy couple who anticipated great financial and professional rewards in exchange for their treasonous, self-serving actions. After Bill graduated from Yale Law School, he was elected Arkansas Attorney General.

Nursing aspirations for world domination, the British Crown set its sights on weakening Germany, whose power, wealth, and technology eclipsed its own.   After Germany fell to defeat through two World Wars, Rothschild conceived the European Coal and Steal Community to enmesh Germany in a series of interlocking dependencies, like NATO, that would keep the Americans in, the Germans down, and the Russians out. Rothschild and other globalists maintained that war was caused by nationalistic impulses, rather than dynastic power grabs, and that enduring peace could only be achieved by eroding sovereignty and tying countries down through foreign obligations and commitments, which, in effect, prevented them from acting in their own interests while allowing international bankers and their agents to determine their fates. This was a strategy Kissinger nursed to great effect.

At the end of World War II, the elites laid the foundation for

China to become a world power. "American diplomats surrendered the territorial integrity and political independence of China (and) wrote the blueprint for the communist conquest of China in a secret agreement at the Yalta (conference)," said Gen. Patrick Hurley, who served as U.S. Ambassador to China.c During World War II, the United States, with the stated intent of helping China fight the Japanese, armed Communist China through the Soviets, who had received U.S. technology to fight Hitler, creating a bonanza for defense contractors.

The New York Sun was critical of America's decision to enter the European wars. "It (is) folly for this country to sacrifice itself to the frenzy of dynastic policies and the clash of ancient hatred which is urging the old world to its destruction," the broadsheet opined in 1914.

The World Wars moved the United States from a position of isolationism and fiscal restraint into nationalism and deficit spending. Newly minted millionaires and billionaires grew out of the ashes of Europe, with the House of Morgan leveraging its connections with the British banking community to broker billions of dollars in transactions.

The income tax was introduced in 1913 as a tax on the wealthy to finance the first World War. After the Japanese bombed Pearl Harbor in 1942, the United States was drawn into World War II. To avoid a deficit, Congress passed the Revenue Act, which *Time* magazine described as "the biggest piece of machinery ever designed to separate dollars from citizens." As *Time* magazine reported,[ci] "The middle class had pitched in before—paying a tax on a purchase was seen as totally normal—but most people had never written a check to Uncle Sam. Now that link would be set in stone....Patriotism—the moral imperative to at least sacrifice dollars while others sacrificed their lives—was enough to carry the Revenue Act through Congress, just as it had carried taxes like the temporary tax imposed during the Civil War. But after World War II, the 1942 tax structure stuck around."

The wars, whether directed against drugs, terrorism, poverty, or illiteracy, all helped expand the federal bureaucracy, transforming the government into a ravenous Leviathan that constantly needed to be fed with taxes.

If the Americans could finance corporate business domestically, why not have them finance the development of the entire world, generating an endless number of taxpayer-supported contracts and effortless wealth for elites, they reasoned. What did taxpayers receive in return? Crumbling infrastructure, failing schools, depleted pension funds,[cii] and a host of other societal ills. While the American middle class bore the brunt of the financial burden, third world countries around the globe were boasting of their newfound prosperity.

***

America's greatest ally in the Middle East, Israel, was used as a tool to facilitate China's rise. Through a series of linkages Kissinger and his ilk had established to perpetuate relationships based upon interdependency, Israel provided weapons to the Shah of Iran in exchange for oil. After the Ayatollah Khomeini assumed power through the Iranian Revolution, Israel lost a buyer for its weapons that it had acquired through U.S. R&D and money. "China could fill the vacuum," Israel concluded, thus opening a channel for Israeli weapons transfers to China.[ciii] In the tradition of the OSS and couriers during the Napoleonic Wars which facilitated communication and intelligence on behalf of the Rothschilds and their agents, Israel's national intelligence agency, the Mossad, was enlisted to train the Shah's Organization of National Intelligence and Security (Savak), to serve as a secret police. The Savak, in turn, gathered intelligence for Iran and the West.

After receiving the Israeli weapons, China passed them along to North Korea, which turned around and threatened the United States and its ally, South Korea, generating billions of dollars more for defense contractors. "War is a racket," affirmed retired U.S. Marine Corps Major General Smedley Butler.

Israel also helped modernize Chinese armed forces through the Talpiot program. Since the collapse of the Soviet Union, Russia has emerged as a leading recipient of Israeli aid, and yet if Israel were America's greatest ally in the Middle East and a leading benefactor of U.S. aid, why was Israel arming America's avowed enemies?

Reflecting the strategy and agenda of the globalists, Israeli Prime Minister Bibi Netanyahu boasted at Fink's Bar in Jerusalem in 1990 that "America is a golden calf, and we will suck it dry, chop it up, and sell it off piece by piece until there is nothing left but the world's biggest welfare state that we will create and control. Why? Because it's the will of God, and America is big enough to take the hit, so we do it again and again and again."[civ]

While the corrupt, degenerate European aristocrats claimed a divine right to rule, no one in their right mind confused them with God. After the United States spent billions of dollars fighting the War on Iraq, Israel became the primary recipient of Iraqi oil, not the United States.[cv] Thanks to U.S. technology transfers, China is pursuing the Belt & Road Initiative in concert with Israel and Russia with a view to usurping America's leadership which emerging as America's greatest strategic threat.

***

To be sure, Communist China was built with American wealth and ingenuity, with the Europeans of old pulling the strings. Following a tried and true pattern, the elites deflected from their own unforgiveable actions onto the West and the United States in order to justify spending more public money to rebalance the scales of justice. As always, the elites who virtue signaled on behalf of their victims, were the leading benefactors of the financial redress that followed.

With a few to opening the United States to China, Arkansas Senator William Fulbright expressed outrage over the indignities China had suffered at the hands of Western imperialists. "China has experienced very little except humiliation in its relations with the West," he told Congress in 1966.[cvi] "The coming of Western civilization to China in the 19th century meant the plundering of China's wealth by foreigners within their own countries... Missionaries ...treating the Chinese as heathens...Western companies destroyed their Chinese competitors in the scale of such products as timber, oil, tobacco, and, of course, opium...Each of China's disastrous nineteenth century wars with the West was followed by the levy of a huge indemnity of some further incursion of the economic life of the country. Why are the Chinese Communist leaders so hostile to the United States and why do they advocate violent revolution against most of the world's governments?"[cvii]

His speech neglected to mention how the Chinese Communist leaders had been propped up by corrupt European elites and their American agents. His proposed solution was not to challenge the supporters of communism, who were hollowing out the spiritual and material substance of the world, but to encourage America to soften its stance against them.

In his testimony, Fulbright advocated opening doors to Communist China in the interests of preserving peace. "China and America may be heading toward war with each other," he said. "It is essential that we do all that can be done to prevent that calamity...It is real because China is ruled by ideological dogmatists who will soon have nuclear weapons at their disposal... (They are) intensely hostile to the United States...The Chinese today, like America a hundred years ago, are in an agitated and abnormal state of mind."

Fulbright would go on to mentor a young Bill Clinton who had clerked for him during his junior year at Georgetown University. The Chinese would later bankroll Clinton's presidential campaign.

The 1960s were a period of great upheaval. Race wars and Marxism raged across university campuses as hippies organized peaceful, pot-filled sit-ins to protest war. As radical ideology took hold in the United States, the younger generation rejected the conventional values of their parents whose work ethic, thrift, morals, and common sense had calcified the backbone of American society.

While the United States fought communists throughout the world, America's politicians couldn't get into bed with them fast enough, including Ted Kennedy, whose family enjoyed a close, personal relationship with the Clintons.

TK's father, Joe Kennedy, had forged a respectable career in politics and finance as Chairman of the U.S. Securities and Exchange Commission and U.S. Ambassador to the United Kingdom. After spending time in European elite circles, he returned to the United States deeply skeptical of the agenda at play. "The whole reason for aiding England is to give us time," he said. "It isn't that (England) is fighting for democracy. That's bunk. She's fighting for self-preservation, just as we will if it comes to us....I know more about the European situation than anybody else."[cviii]

He was right, of course. England was concerned about challenging German power. Once the United States entered the war, the transnational networks were allowed access into American political institutions. Ambassador Kennedy would never have the opportunity to warn the American people as he was relieved from his post shortly after making these remarks.

His son, President John F. Kennedy sought to burnish his father's legacy. In remarks before the American Newspaper Publishers

Association on April 27, 1961 at the Waldorf-Astoria Hotel in New York City, JFK clearly identifies the danger posed by the Deep State:

"You may remember that in 1851, the *New York Herald Tribune* under the sponsorship and publishing of Horace Greeley employed as its London correspondent an obscure journalist by the name of Karl Marx.

"We are told that foreign correspondent Marx, stone broke and with a family ill and undernourished, constantly appealed to Greeley and managing editor Charles Dana for an increase in his munificent salary of $5 per installment, a salary which he and Engels ungratefully labeled as the 'lousiest petty bourgeois cheating'."

"But when all his financial appeals were refused, Marx looked around for other means of livelihood and fame, eventually terminating his relationship with the *Tribune* and devoting his talents full time to the cause that would bequeath the world the seeds of Leninism, Stalinism, revolution, and the Cold War.

"If only this capitalistic New York newspaper had treated him more kindly; if only Marx had remained a foreign correspondent, history might have been different. And I hope all publishers will bear this lesson in mind the next time they receive a poverty-stricken appeal for a small increase in the expense account from an obscure newspaper man....

"The events of recent weeks may have helped to illuminate that challenge for some; but the dimensions of its threat have loomed large on the horizon for many years. Whatever our hopes may be for the future--for reducing this threat or living with it--there is no escaping either the gravity or the totality of its challenge to our survival and to our security--a challenge that confronts us in unaccustomed ways in every sphere of human activity.

"This deadly challenge imposes upon our society two requirements of direct concern both to the press and to the President-- two requirements that may seem almost contradictory in tone, but which must be reconciled and fulfilled if we are to meet this national peril. I refer, first, to the need for far greater public information; and, second, to the need for far greater official secrecy.

"The very word 'secrecy' is repugnant in a free and open society; and we, as a people, are inherently and historically opposed to secret societies, to secret oaths, and to secret proceedings.

"We decided long ago that the dangers of excessive and

unwarranted concealment of pertinent facts far outweighs the dangers which are cited to justify it. Even today, there is little value in opposing the threat of a closed society by imitating its arbitrary restrictions.

"Even today, there is little value in insuring the survival of our nation if our traditions do not survive with it. And there is very grave danger that an announced need for increased security will be seized upon by those anxious to expand its meaning to the very limits of official censorship and concealment.

"That I do not intend to permit to the extent that it is in my control. And no official of my Administration, whether his rank is high or low, civilian or military, should interpret my words here tonight as an excuse to censor the news, to stifle dissent, to cover up our mistakes or to withhold from the press and the public the facts they deserve to know.

"But I do ask every publisher, every editor, and every newsman in the nation to reexamine his own standards, and to recognize the nature of our country's peril. In time of war, the government and the press have customarily joined in an effort based largely on self-discipline, to prevent unauthorized disclosures to the enemy. In time of 'clear and present danger,' the courts have held that even the privileged rights of the First Amendment must yield to the public's need for national security.

"Today no war has been declared--and however fierce the struggle may be, it may never be declared in the traditional fashion. Our way of life is under attack. Those who make themselves our enemy are advancing around the globe. The survival of our friends is in danger. And yet no war has been declared, no borders have been crossed by marching troops, no missiles have been fired.

"If the press is awaiting a declaration of war before it imposes the self-discipline of combat conditions, then I can only say that no war ever posed a greater threat to our security. If you are awaiting a finding of 'clear and present danger,' then I can only say that the danger has never been more clear and its presence has never been more imminent.

"It requires a change in outlook, a change in tactics, a change in missions--by the government, by the people, by every businessman or labor leader, and by every newspaper. For we are opposed around the world by a monolithic and ruthless conspiracy that relies primarily on covert means for expanding its sphere of influence--on infiltration instead of invasion, on subversion instead of elections, on intimidation instead of free choice, on guerrillas by night instead of armies by day. It is a system which has conscripted vast human and material resources into the building of a tightly knit, highly efficient machine that combines military, diplomatic, intelligence, economic, scientific, and political operations.

"Its preparations are concealed, not published. Its mistakes are buried, not headlined. Its dissenters are silenced, not praised. No expenditure is questioned, no rumor is printed, no secret is revealed. It conducts the Cold War, in short, with a war-time discipline no democracy would ever hope or wish to match.

"Nevertheless, every democracy recognizes the necessary restraints of national security--and the question remains whether those restraints need to be more strictly observed if we are to oppose this kind of attack as well as outright invasion.

"For the facts of the matter are that this nation's foes have openly boasted of acquiring through our newspapers information they would otherwise hire agents to acquire through theft, bribery or espionage; that details of this nation's covert preparations to counter the enemy's covert operations have been available to every newspaper reader, friend and foe alike; that the size, the strength, the location and the nature of our forces and weapons, and our plans and strategy for their use, have all been pinpointed in the press and other news media to a degree sufficient to satisfy any foreign power; and that, in at least in one case, the publication of details concerning a secret mechanism whereby satellites were followed required its alteration at the expense of considerable time and money.

"The newspapers which printed these stories were loyal, patriotic, responsible and well-meaning. Had we been engaged in open warfare, they undoubtedly would not have published such items. But in the absence of open warfare, they recognized only the tests of journalism and not the tests of national security. And my question tonight is whether additional tests should not now be adopted....

"On many earlier occasions, I have said--and your newspapers have constantly said--that these are times that appeal to every citizen's sense of sacrifice and self-discipline. They call out to every citizen to weigh his rights and comforts against his obligations to the common good. I cannot now believe that those citizens who serve in the newspaper business consider themselves exempt from that appeal.

"It is the unprecedented nature of this challenge that also gives rise to your second obligation--an obligation which I share. And that is our obligation to inform and alert the American people--to make certain that they possess all the facts that they need and understand them as well--the perils, the prospects, the purposes of our program and the choices that we face.

"No President should fear public scrutiny of his program. For from that scrutiny comes understanding; and from that understanding comes support or opposition. And both are necessary. I am not asking your newspapers to support the Administration, but I am asking your help in the tremendous task of informing and alerting the American people. For I have complete confidence in the response and dedication of our citizens whenever they are fully informed.

"This means greater coverage and analysis of international news--for it is no longer far away and foreign but close at hand and local. It means greater attention to improved understanding of the news as well as improved transmission. And it means, finally, that government at all levels, must meet its obligation to provide you with the fullest possible information outside the narrowest limits of national security--and we intend to do it.

"It was early in the Seventeenth Century that Francis Bacon remarked on three recent inventions already transforming the world: the compass, gunpowder and the printing press. Now the links between the nations first forged by the compass have made us all citizens of the world, the hopes and threats of one becoming the hopes and threats of us all. In that one world's efforts to live together, the evolution of gunpowder to its ultimate limit has warned mankind of the terrible consequences of failure.

"And so it is to the printing press--to the recorder of man's deeds, the keeper of his conscience, the courier of his news--that we look for strength and assistance, confident that with your help, man will be what he was born to be: free and independent."

Willfully ignoring JFK's admonitions, instead of serving as faithful guardians of the Fourth Estate, the media has peddled obfuscation, misinformation, race baiting, and celebrity voyeurism, very little of which feeds the soul, engages the intellect, spurs thoughtful dialog, or holds the powerful in check. It's meaningless distraction and empty marketing that has rendered national dialog vacuous and divisive.

While the media had become a faithful lapdog to elite interests, the Smith-Mundt Act made it illegal for the federal government to disseminate propaganda to domestic audiences. This changed during the Obama Administration which authorized "the domestic dissemination of information and material about the United States intended primarily for foreign audiences, and for other purposes."[cix]

Perhaps wishing to avert the fate of his assassinated brother, Ted Kennedy, who nursed Presidential ambitions of his own, was quick to align with the interests of Deep State. If his noble brother sought to save the Republic, TK was quick to hasten its demise.

In order to conquer the United States, the enemy would have to subvert it from within by undermining its values, neutralizing its strength, weakening its resolve, plundering its assets, and hollowing out its institutions.

TK's treachery began with his unrestrained support for the Immigration and Nationality Act of 1965, which ended the immigration quota system and removed restrictions on immediate relations of immigrants. Previously, the American immigration system gave priority to Northern and Western European immigrants who shared the values and culture of the United States. In contrast, Kennedy opened the doors to Africa and Asia, where communists were fomenting revolutions.

The bill was written by Norbert Schell, a legal adviser to Kennedy whose client list included Atlantic Richfield and business interests in Asia.

Recall Kissinger's discussions with Mao in which the men privately discussed "flooding" the country with Chinese immigrants for the specific purpose of impairing the interests of the United States and "let(ting) in so many nationalities."

While Americans have begun to resist the influx of immigrants into this country, their resistance was not based upon racism. Kissinger remarked effusively about tolerance Americans expressed towards people from other lands. The new immigrants elites sought to bring into the United States were those whom knew would deliberately create problems for the host country and impair its interests. It is difficult for Americans to believe that the immigration laws were written with this intent, but the elites have admitted to this in their own words, and the problems created as a result are palpable.

According to NumbersUSA, an organization that seeks to reduce legal and illegal immigration into the United States, Kennedy's immigration policies have "fundamentally changed America" by destroying the ability of the United States to control its own borders and be an environmentally sustainable nation. Immigrants are now coming into the country faster than they can be absorbed, inflicting stress on communities and impairing their ability to meet budgets due to growing demands for medical care, education, housing, and social services. In turn, Americans are facing dramatic increases in property taxes, making it difficult for many to purchase and maintain their own homes. Hundreds of thousands of Americans have fallen out of the middle class as their occupations have collapsed and their wages have stagnated while their taxes had shot into the stratosphere.[cx]

In the 1970s, Kennedy expanded the refugee program, spawning a resettlement cottage industry. As public funds became available for refugees and other poor immigrants, corporations demanded the United States increase its intake of poor, unskilled immigrants to exploit cheap labor, in turn displacing more American from jobs while increasing the demand for more public housing and entitlement programs for the needy which government contractors provided, making elites richer at the expense of ordinary citizens. Americans who have taken umbrage with this self serving agenda have been disparaged as racists, nationalists, and part of old America that deserves to die, not unlike the traditional Chinese whose noble culture and religion were decimated by the materialistic communists who seized control in their country.

The government has further accommodated Big Business at the expense of ordinary citizens by ensuring corporations receive subsidies and tax relief to hire foreigners over Americans, often paying immigrants lower wages than what their American counterparts would need to survive. The taxpayers are then required to support poor immigrants to make up the wage differential. The more needy, unskilled, and vulnerable the people that can be brought into the country, the more government contractors and corporations can profit by way of providing them free or subsidized housing, new schools, hospitals, equipment, products, and services that are taxpayer subsidized, with churches, mosques, and synagogues receiving lucrative government contracts in exchange for providing hospitality to needy immigrants.

Kennedy tried to force through more immigration legislation between 2000 and 2008, creating a lottery that randomly gave away 50,000 green cards a year to people in countries with the least cultural ties and affinity with the United States, some of which sponsored terrorism. Elites profited from the influx while consolidating power through the societal chaos that ensued.

TK also pushed the H-1B visa for immigrants with specialized knowledge, preventing hundreds of thousands of American children from acquiring jobs in high tech companies. He further helped squash the recommendations of Civil Rights activist Barbara Jordan's Blue Ribbon Commission to reduce overall immigration and eliminate chain migration and the immigration lottery.[cxi] He even promoted mini amnesties directed as specific nationalities, transforming the United States permanently while residing near the Chinese Embassy in the posh neighborhood of Kalorama in Washington, DC.

Between 1966 and 1979, Ted Kennedy played a critical role behind the scenes in normalizing diplomatic relations with China by "(leading) the electorate out of its hostility and fear of what was then called Red China."[cxii] While angling to be President, he gave speeches that encouraged the United States to build a closer relationship with Communist China. In the spring of 1971, he tried to become the first U.S. politician to travel to China while advocating for full U.S. diplomatic relations with Communist China. Soon after his career took flight, he pleaded guilty to leaving the scene of a car accident that killed his passenger, Mary Jo Kopechne at Chappaquiddick.

TK believed carrying water for the Chinese would be his ticket to the White House. In 1977, he delivered a major foreign policy speech in which he advocated normalizing relations with China before the World Affairs Council of Boston. *The New York Times* described his speech as "the most forthright and detailed proposal made by a politician."

Later that year, TK traveled to China to meet with Deng Ziaoping to discuss an "imaginative and practical" strategy to normalize Sino-U.S. relations The following year, China and the United States had restored diplomatic relations.[cxiii]

When cozying up to the Chinese didn't produce the results he wanted, Ted Kennedy enlisted the help of the Soviets to clear the way for his path to the White House in 1988.[cxiv] As the *London Times* reported in 1992, TK offered to help the Soviets influence the 1984 election through an intermediary Soviet KGB agent. "Kennedy would arm Soviet officials with explanations regarding problems of nuclear disarmament, so they may be better prepared and more convincing during appearances in the USA," the *Washington Post*'s Bob Woodward wrote in the *London Times*. In exchange, Kennedy enlisted Soviet assistance to challenge Ronald Reagan's re-election campaign by offering to use his influential friends in the media to soften the image of Soviet leaders and depict the duly elected President of the United States as "reckless" and "dangerous."

***

By the 1970s, Canadian Prime Minister Pierre Trudeau restored diplomatic relations between Canada and China, giving the Communists access to the North American market and influential Americans.

In 1973, David Rockefeller gathered executives from 300 major U.S. corporations with the founder of China International Trust Investment Corp (CITIC), a Communist China state owned investment company established in 1979 with the approval of Deng Xiopeng, to help North American companies gain access to Chinese markets.

In 1979, the Communist Red Flag was hoisted over the South Lawn of the White House to welcome Deng Xiaoping, signaling a reversal of decades long U.S. opposition to China.

In 1983, when the United States was immersed in the Cold War fighting communism and school children were learning how to hide under desks to protect themselves from the fallout of nuclear war, America industry, including General Motors, Chrysler, Boeing, and Caterpillar were seeking cheap labor and entering emerging markets in China and elsewhere to improve shareholder value.

President Ronald Reagan opened the door further Israel for the purposes of intelligence sharing and technology transfers. Israel promptly passed the technology along to China and Russia, reducing America's global technological advantage and power on the world stage.

In 1985, Reagan signed the U.S.-Israeli Free Trade Agreement which lowered trade barriers between the two countries. The USIFTA was the only free trade agreement ever signed by the United States that did not include provisions for intellectual property rights. The bill was introduced in Congress by Representative James Wright, a Democrat from Texas who had intervened on Charles Keating's behalf in the Savings and Loan crisis that cost taxpayers over $130,000,000,000.

***

Pastor Lindsey Williams revealed that Yale bonesman George H.W. Bush salivated over the vast, untapped markets of China with a view to enriching himself and his globalist friends. An intergenerational beneficiary of corporate welfare, Bush perceived that corporations could profit from China's cheap labor and unlimited market for corporate goods and services that could be sold in the United States and China.

Bush had been a lifelong water carrier for elite interests. After serving as Director of the Liaison Office to the People's Republic of China and as U.S. Ambassador to the United Nations, he became Director of the CIA. A champion of globalism, Bush unveiled his plans for a new world order in his 1991 State of the Union Speech.

"What is at stake is more than one small country, " he said. "It is a big idea: a new world order, where diverse nations are drawn together in common cause to achieve the universal aspirations of mankind–peace and security, freedom, and the rule of law....

"The end of the cold war has been a victory for all humanity.

"A year and a half ago, in Germany, I said that our goal was a Europe whole and free.

"Tonight, Germany is united. Europe has become whole and free, and America's leadership was instrumental....

"The world can, therefore, seize this opportunity to fulfill the long-held promise of a new world order, where brutality will go unrewarded and aggression will meet collective resistance...."

The following year Bush signed an executive order for "the disposition or transfer of an infrastructure asset (to foreign interests) such as by sale or long term lease from state or local government, such as roads, tunnels, bridges, power supply facilities, mass transit, prisons, airports, schools, waterways, mass transit, airports, ports, schools."[cxv]

This needed to be done, Bush explained, so that the United States could achieve "the most beneficial economic use of its resources... for the functioning of the economy."

During the subsequent Administrations of Bill Clinton, George W. Bush, and Barack Obama, the United States placed ports, supermarket chains, uranium supplies, land, and a myriad other national treasures on the international market. Quietly elites began dismantling the United States and selling off its assets to foreign interests.

In the summer of 1990, the Russian Union of Industrialists and Entrepreneurs was established to advance Russian-U.S. public-private sector collaborations. Its founder, Arkady Volsky, had presided over the USSR's military industrial complex and served as the Communist Party's top representative in a car plant in Moscow. Among the key executives of the group were Igor Yurgens, an advisor to UNESCO who had worked for the International Institute for Strategic Studies, a foreign policy think tank that has received money from Russia and China. A "certified Marxist," Yurgens presided over Renaissance Capital, which paid Bill Clinton $500,000 in speaking fees.[cxvi]

The U.S.-Russian Business Council was then formed, establishing offices in Moscow and Washington, DC. After extending membership to Kissinger Associates, the group boasted on its website that it group enjoys "excellent relations with both the United States and Russian governments" along with "unparalleled and timely access to policy makers" and "leverage with members of the legislative and executive branches" in both Russian and the United States. The USRBC helped establish U.S. Permanent Normal Trade Relations with Russia.

As Bush campaigned for re-election, a maverick billionaire by the name of Ross Perot challenged him as an independent. During his campaign for the Presidency, Perot warned the American people about the perils of globalism, particularly the North American Free Trade Agreement that he predicted would result in a "giant sucking sound" of American jobs to Mexico and Latin America. The diminutive Perot who had a commanding presence and loud voice, split the vote, enabling another globalist, Bill Clinton, to win the White House. As President, Clinton presided over the disastrous NAFTA agreement crafted by the Mexican-U.S. Business Committee which was co-chaired by Rodman Clark Rockefeller, the eldest son of Nelson Rockefeller who had served on the Board of the Rockefeller Brothers.

Bill and Hillary Clinton were arguably more ruthless than Bush in their implementation of the globalist agenda. Larry Nichols, who had worked closely with Gov. Bill Clinton in Arkansas,[cxvii] said that the Clintons "dealt with the Progressive Council which was innately more prestigious than the Council of Foreign Relations. By that I'm saying that their dedication is to destroy the Government of the United States....The Clintons were eager to fulfill the demands of the Council of Foreign Relations. They were absolutely happy to deliver whatever they needed as long as they supported their Progressive Council. You're not going to find much information about them as they don't want to be located. They are a covert operation. These people don't want to be acknowledged. They don't want to be talked about...They don't want to be known....When people like me dare to talk, there is considerable risk involved in doing it....My motive in doing it is that it's my country they are trying to destroy, and I want to save it."[cxviii]

Bill Clinton was elected Governor of Arkansas twice, though not in succession. As a young man, he clerked for Fulbright and cultivated Arkansas Gov. Winthrop Rockefeller who combated allegations of cronyism and corruption that mirrored the Clintons' political ascent. Among Rockefeller's critics was Osro Cobb, who lost out on a Rhodes Scholarship to Fulbright. While Cobb would go on to a short-lived appointment to the Arkansas Supreme Court, Fulbright enjoyed an illustrious career as U.S. Senator. In his memoirs,[cxix] Cobb wrote that Rockefeller " had used ruthless tactics to convert the fine Republican state organization into a one-man Rockefeller machine, loyal not to party but to Rockefeller personally. In rapid succession, Mr. Rockefeller captiously took over most of the functions of the state chairman and in a matter of months succeeded in taking over and exercising absolute right of dictation as to each and every important party function at the state level. Such one-man dictatorship is clearly the deadly enemy of any semblance of two-party government. ... Faithful Republican leaders who have worked tirelessly over the years have been pushed aside or replaced."

With powerful advocates in his corner, Clinton leaped from the governorship to the White House, though he arguably would not made this jump had it not be for the money he received from Communist China.

In 1993, a DNC fundraiser was caught making arrangements for a representative of a Chinese Weapons Trading Company to meet Clinton, who was offering appointments to U.S. trade missions in exchange for campaign contributions. Among Clinton's appointments to the Commerce Department was a suspected Communist Chinese agent who gathered military and economic intelligence, including satellite encryption, for Red China.[cxx] Not only was Communist China among the largest contributors to the Clinton-Gore campaign in 1992, but *The Washington Post* revealed that the People's Republic of China donated money to the DNC to help Clinton win re-election in 1997.

After receiving a deluge of money from the Chinese, Clinton promoted China's entry into the World Trade Organization. Most Democrats, who received campaign contributions from unions, opposed his efforts over valid concerns that workers would lose jobs to outsourcing and cheap labor if China were to join the WTO. Christians and conservatives opposed engaging the murderous, Godless Communists while high tech companies were keen to enter the lucrative Chinese market to increase shareholder value.

To secure China's interests, the Clinton's reached out to their leading ally in the House of Representatives, Congressman Tom DeLay, whom the *New York Times* characterized as "the President's chief water carrier and potential legacy builder in an all out battle to grant China permanent normal trade privileges to allow companies to benefit fully from a market opening accord that paves the way for China's entry into the WTO."[cxxi]

DeLay, who aggressively solicited corporate campaign contributions, delivered the votes Clinton needed in the House of Representatives. "We talked about what each of us has to do, and we gave each other advice," DeLay told reporters.

China's entry into the WTO was also supported by Federal Reserve Chairman Alan Greenspan and Presidents Ford, Carter, and Bush, who each provided a letter of support at the request of President Bill Clinton.

"Exporting American values undermines the Communist regime in China," DeLay said, justifying his betrayal of America. "Free market principles, entrepreneurship, the Internet, all their institutions reflect American values. I see it as the beginning of the end of Communism."

Instead it the beginning of the end of the United States. While wrapping himself in the flag, DeLay never considered values as a bargaining ploy. Discussions between the two countries didn't focus on democratic principles, human rights, God or rule of law, but on weapons transfers, market access, and money – values DeLay could appreciate as the chief organizer of the K Street Project which ensured that corporate money was directed his way to finance his own personal fiefdom on Capitol Hill.

It would not be long before the feds were investigating Clinton on multiple fronts, from his sexual dalliances with women, like intern Monica Lewinsky, who may have compromised national security, to the improper influence of Chinese money on the Administration's policies. As scandals engulfed the Clinton White House, DeLay mobilized Republicans to impeach Clinton but not for the reasons one might think. Despite having betrayed his own marital vows, DeLay argued that Clinton should be impeached on grounds that he "(lacked) the necessary moral authority to protect U.S. interests in the world," based on his affair with Lewinsky.

Two days before the House of Representatives impeachment hearings got underway, Admiral Thomas Moorer, a former Chairman of the Joint Chiefs of Staff, pleaded with DeLay to highlight Chinagate and the role of Clinton's "betrayal of our security."cxxii

As Moorer explained, "President Clinton promised to restrain those who ordered the Tiananmen Square massacre but has now allowed these men whose hands are stained with the blood of martyrs to freedom into the highest reaches of our military defenses and made available to them significant portions of our Administration's technology, giving the Red Chinese a controlling presence in Panama...to the point where it could someday neutralize our entire deployed military capability."

Moorer observed that DeLay ignored his entreaties and proceeded to allow the Clintons to define the terms of the impeachment inquiry. A personal friend of the Clintons, DeLay chose to focus on Clinton's sex with an intern instead of Chinagate. The Clintons would later reciprocate by having federal prosecutors drop their corruption charges against DeLay while he was working with a producer recommended by the Clintons to spin the story surrounding his political downfall through a reality TV show that would generate untold wealth for him and facilitate his political comeback. Sadly for DeLay, who overvalued his own personal appeal and importance to elites, there were no takers for his show.

Attorney General Janet Reno refused to investigate Chinagate but readily allowed Ken Starr's investigation of Lewinsky to proceed, thereby distracting from it. As Edward Timperlake and William

Triplett reported in <u>Year of the Rat: How Bill Clinton Compromised U.S. Security for Chinese Cash</u>, Clinton single handedly erased the U.S. strategic and military advantage over the Chicoms by releasing nuclear secrets to them.

In 2001, a meeting of the World Trade Organization welcomed China as its 148th member, with Chinese President Jiang Zemin promising to "strike a carefully thought out balance between honoring its commitment and enjoying its rights."

By then, George W. Bush was President.

As China's lucrative markets opened up, Neil Bush scored a five-year consulting contract worth $2,000,000 with Grace Semiconductors Manufacturing Corp while Bill Clinton and Sam Walton increased contracts with Chinese factories over 2000 percent leading to a trade imbalance. As Hillary Clinton prepared for her first run for the Presidency, Alibaba, China's answer to Amazon, donated $250,000 to the Clinton Foundation in 2006; other companies, including Microsoft, HSBC, and CitiGroup, made their own generous donations for market access and deals with China. Having served as a loyal hand maiden to globalists, Hillary Clinton campaigning hard to win the White House in 2008. When she lost to Obama, she tried again in 2016 after having cozied up to foreign interests and sold access to the federal government through the Clinton Foundation during her tenure as Secretary of State. Despite her eagerness to betray her own country for untold riches and power, Hillary's career ended in disgrace.

***

The second President George W. Bush continued his father's legacy by parceling off the United States to foreign interests. For example, six major U.S. ports were transferred to United Arab Emirates-owned and operated companies. America's roads, bridges, and airlinescxxiii were even auctioned off on international markets, with citizens balking at paying tolls to use roads that were suddenly owned by foreign interests.

The *Trucker's Report* raised concerns that "in a short-sighted attempt to fill holes in their budgets, some states have been selling control over their toll roads to private foreign investors." For example, Indiana Toll road's 75-year lease that started in 2006 has doubled tolls for five axle trucks.cxxiv "Few people know that tolls from the U.S.

side of the tunnel between Detroit and Windsor, Canada, go to a subsidiary of an Australian company which also owns a bridge in Alabama," the Associated Press reported. "Some experts welcome the trend (as) private investors can raise more money than politicians to build new roads because these kind of owners are willing to raise tolls."[cxxv]

In 2006, *WND* reporter Jerome Corsi observed that "The Department of Transportation, acting under President Bush's orders, is preparing to issue an administrative ruling that would open U.S. airlines to foreign ownership despite specific prohibitions and warnings from Congress."

There was no question that globalist meddling in American policy had undermined America's security, sovereignty, and economic strength. The terrorist attacks on the World Trade Center and Pentagon on September 11, 2001 symbolized the decline of the United States as a world power.

While civil liberties were being eroded in the United States, which was squandering treasure and sacrificing lives on wars in Iraq and Afghanistan, globalists were prospering through opportunities in China. Among the beneficiaries was Silverstein Properties, a real estate firm that developed and managed the World Trade Center. After the WTC fell, Silverstein Properties, Inc. received a $2,000,000,000 settlement in 2007 on top of the $2,550,000,000 already paid by insurers to resolve outstanding claims for the building. Seven years later, Silverstein Properties bid $2,210,000,000 for an undeveloped site in Qianhai, an emerging Chinese free trade zone in which "China (was) preparing to test a freer flow of the yuan in and out of the country."[cxxvi]

A few years after terrorists struck the Twin Towers, Chi Haotian, the Vice Chairman of China's Military Commission threatened to nuke hundreds of American cities so that China could expand into the United States on grounds of "racial superiority" and "eminent domain." The North American continent belonged to them anyway, he said, as Native Americans had immigrated from China and therefore the Chinese were the first Americans. To accomplish this plan, the United States would need to be "cleansed" of between 150,000,000 and 200,000,000 Americans through biological weapons.[cxxvii] It was not right, he said, that Americans should enjoy so much open space when China was overpopulated and crowded. Yet, while Chinese leaders were speaking of exterminating U.S. citizens, American multinationals continued to rush in to do business with China in a quest for the Almighty renminbi.

During Bush's final year in office, the global economy collapsed, spurred by a crisis in the subprime mortgage market, leading to more taxpayer-supported bailouts for Wall Street. On October 3, 2008, that amount approached $700,000,000,000. Seven years later, the Special Inspector General for (the Troubled Asset Relief Program) revealed that the bailout had committed the federal government to $16,800,000,000,000 in addition to the $4,600,000,000,000 already paid out. "Yes, it was trillions, not billions, and the banks are now larger and still too big to fail," *Forbes* reported. "But it isn't just the government bailout money that tells the story of the bailout. This is a story about lies, cheating, and a multi-faceted corruption which was often criminal."cxxviii

***

While promising "hope and change" on the campaign trail, President Barack Obama reached across the aisle to link hands with the traitorous Republicans to ram through the TransPacific Partnership through Congress. The bill was slated to allow unrestricted immigration into the United States to fulfill jobs and facilitate trade among the nations in the Pacific. NAFTA-style international tribunals were to be established to override American law in the event of trade disputes. Curtis Ellis, the Executive Director of the American Jobs Alliance,cxxix told the *Hill* newspaper that the Transpacific Partnership also included an entire chapter on immigration. "It is a Trojan Horse for Obama's immigration agenda," he said. "The House Members were ready to defund the Department of Homeland Security to stop President Obama's Executive Action on unrestricted immigration to fill jobs and trade among nations in the Pacific." The TPP was prepared to surrender constitutionally delegated authority over trade to Obama vis-à-vis a Fast Track authority that included a domestically expanded and temporary workers program.

Despite having spent five years trying to persuade Congress to approve TPP and receiving fawning support from Ohio Governor John Kasich and billionaire Michael Bloomberg, the legislation died in Committee. The TPP stood to enrich multinationals further, shore up cheap labor, and open new markets for business while stripping Congress of its authority to restrict immigration into the United States. In effect, the free flow of immigration would have been allowed among signatory nations, similar to the European Union's Schengen Agreement, which guarantees free movement of people throughout the European continent. Among the signatories were Canada, Mexico, Australia, New Zealand, Chile, Peru, with Communist China expected to sign on later.

Luckily for the American people, the TPP was scrapped on grounds of unconstitutionality, given that it stood to repeal enumerated powers granted to Congress in Article 1 of the Constitution to regulate immigration. It also would have allowed jobs available to U.S. workers to be given to foreign workers instead resulting in widespread unemployment for American citizens. The globalist aspired to a borderless North American union similar to that which was unfolding on the European continent. The TPP was to be subsumed into a larger planned Free Trade Area of the Asia Pacific which included Communist China and Russia, for a FTAAP, whose long term goal was to link Pacific Rim economies from China to Chile to the United States through regional and bilateral free trade agreements.

As Secretary of State, Hillary Rodham Clinton played the role of international saleswoman, inviting Russian government officials to sign a multi-billion dollar deal to buy dozens of aircraft from Boeing. A month later, Clinton was in China, where she jubilantly announced that Boeing would be writing a generous check to help resuscitate floundering U.S. efforts to host a pavilion at the upcoming World Fair. Boeing, she boasted, "has just agreed to double its contribution to $2,000,000." Boeing donated $900,000 to the William J. Clinton Foundation two months after securing a $3,700,000,000 deal in Russia, the *Washington Post* reported in 2010.cxxx

While selling her office to the highest bidder, Hillary reportedly violated ethics guidelines that prohibited her as Secretary of State from soliciting business for Boeing in exchange for donations to her private charity. As a agent of the Crown with longstanding ties to the CIA, she needn't worry about consequences. Quickly this scandal would be swept under the rug, just as all the others had, and she'd persevere, doing as she had always done.

***

The United States was not always such an easy mark. Rolling out the public relations offensive on behalf of China was the National Committee on United States-China Relations. The National Committee did not concern itself with the best interests of the United States nor did it champion values or principles, beyond wanting to enrich elites and their networks through Communist China. In his transcripts, Henry Kissinger makes it very clear that the United States would not try to reform or bring Western principles to any foreign country. What mattered to elites were profits and *realpolitik.*

"It is no exaggeration to assert that the National Committee played a major role in enabling the issue of China to be viewed in all its full complexity with policies examined with respect to American interests," said Bob Scalapino, the Committee's first Chairman.cxxxi

The first National Committee opened in the Library of the Church at the United Nations building in New York in 1966. Among its financial supporters were the Sloan Foundation (General Motors) and John D. Rockefeller, III. From the beginning, the group sought to "reach all segments of American society from the laymen to the specialist to the policy maker. It must also keep abreast of continuing developments in China, tap the available sources of knowledge, and forge enduring links between appropriate national organizations, information outlets, secondary and higher educational institutions, America-China specialists and those abroad."

Thanks in no small part to the National Committee, Nixon became the first president to normalize U.S.-China relations. In turn, Boeing, a leading U.S. defense contractor, was able to secure new markets by introducing its aircraft to China and developing the Chinese air transportation system. Boeing has since established a relationship with the Chinese airlines aviation industry and Chinese government. Pfizer, the largest pharmaceutical company in China opened shop there in 1980. Drugs subsequently marketed to American citizens have been accompanied with strange, and often debilitating side effects. One medicine might combat heart disease, for example, while spurring blindness or cancer. If the Federal Drug Administration were truly vetting pharmaceuticals, would such drugs be allowed to be sold and distributed to American citizens?

All that mattered to elites were profits and shoring up their advantage against everyone else, which necessarily meant weakening those who could challenge them.

It's hard to imagine that a little over a half a century ago, doing business with China would have been unthinkable. After the World Wars, President Harry S. Truman went so far as to sign an executive order to screen federal employees for their association with organizations that were "Totalitarian, Fascist, Communist, or subversive" or which sought to "alter the form of Government of the United States by unconstitutional means." He understood the threat the United States faced at the hands of Communists and tried to protect his country like a True Man. In the 1950s, Sen. Joe McCarthy raised the alarm that Communists had infiltrated the State Department, spurring a communist witch hunt that ensnared a number of federal government employees and Hollywood talent in its net.

At the end of World War II in 1945, China joined the United Nations. Eight years later, William F. Buckley's protégé, Marvin Liebman, the co-founder of Young Americans for Freedom and the American Conservative Union, launched One Million Against the Admission of Communist China into the United Nations. Buckley, a bonesman who is credited with the modern conservative movement, warned in God and Man at Yale that Christianity in America was straying from its essence and being replaced by another God, one of materialism. "McCarthyism .... is a movement around which men of good will and stern morality can close ranks," Buckley said.

Despite efforts to stall the rise of China, One Million closed its doors after the PRC joined the UN Security Council in 1971, thanks in no small part to the National Committee.

In 1964, Senator William Fulbright, the Chairman of the Senate Foreign Relations Committee, raised the question of whether the United States should introduce "an element of flexibility" into its approach to China. The federal government dismissed Fulbright's arguments, leading globalists to take more dramatic actions to mobilize support for China.

The National Committee brought together the nation's premier academics, economists, intellectuals, journalists, and government officials to create an echo chamber of sorts that would soften the nation's position on China. During the War on Poverty when reckless, unabashed entitlement spending was driving up the national debt, the Committee briefed President Lyndon B. Johnson on ways to improve U.S.-Chinese relations. As word traveled around Capitol Hill that supporting China could engender support for political campaigns among the well heeled, corporate classes, ambitious politicians rushed to accommodate China, including, for example, Ted Kennedy and John Edwards, both of whom nursed aspirations to become President.

Time magazine publisher and Skull & Bones member Henry Luce, who had worked with AIG founder Cornelius Vander Starr and the OSS decades earlier, was eager to weigh in on the China question too. "China will account for half the population of the whole world," he told audiences. "We must soon find ways of living at peace with half the human race or your generation will know nothing but endless war in the Orient....What argument can be made for our present policy of trading with the Russians or selling them wheat that cannot be made for trading with Red China and feeding her far more desperate people?"

The Saturday Evening Post followed up with an editorial entitled, "Let's Open the Door to China," that incorporated Luce's remarks.

In 1964, World Trade Association President Jack Gompers advocated launching a business committee to "explore trade possibilities with the People's Republic of China."cxxxii After Gompers' remarks were widely denounced, the National Committee redouble its efforts.

The National Committee convinced the U.S. Chamber of Commerce to recommend "steps designed to more effectively open channels of communication with the people of mainland China." The Chamber then published a book entitled A New China Policy: Some Quaker Proposals, which called for America's full recognition of the People's Republic of China.cxxxiii

The liberal League of Women Voters was similarly tapped to select China as a study issue for its chapters scattered throughout the United States.

Through a gradual process of indoctrination, the American public were led down a fool's path into believing that it was in America's interests to forge a closer relationship with Communist China.

Thanks to the efforts of the National Committee by 1965, "China was an issue to be addressed out loud, not whispered with a glance over the shoulder," the group boasted.

That year, the House Foreign Affairs Subcommittee published a report on the status of U.S. China Policy, which a May 22, 1965

Washington Post editorial praised as "a cautious, but courageous step in becoming the first Congressional Group to publish a report (for) consideration (for) limited, but direct, contact with Red China through cultural exchanges," with priority for these exchanges granted to journalists and scholars, who were considered to be influencers and thought leaders. As the Committee observed, journalists could be counted on to be "advocates for change."

The National Committee also tapped World Affairs Councils, the National Council of Churches, Unions, the Ford Foundation, and a host of other globalist organizations to support panel discussions in concert with the United Nations Association to generate reports that "made discussions of rapprochement with China politically respectable."

In order for rapprochement with China to be considered respectable, respectable people would need to support it. To this end, the Committee sought a "broad political spectrum" of supporters, that excluded "those of the extreme left or right. Anyone too battle scarred from the McCarthy era – i.e., outed as Communists – or connected with the anti-China lobby – were excluded to eliminate extremes." Elected officials were barred from membership to avoid "souring political preferences and to avoid being affected by the vicissitudes of political popularity."

On March 20-21, 1969, the National Committee hosted academics, business leaders, journalists, and government officials in New York to discuss the future of China. Sen. Ted Kennedy appeared as a banquet speaker, regaling his audience with proposals to alter America's China policy. Soon after, President Richard Nixon was on his way to normalize relations with China, with the American public cheering him on.

In 1976, the National Committee boasted about its "deep roots in conducting exchanges for members of Congress and their staff." Its 2007 *Annual Report* acknowledged that the Committee held briefings with Navy offices to "balance existing knowledge of military and security matters with economic, domestic politics, environmental challenges, and culture" to help American military leaders "communicate with Chinese counterparts looking to the next generation of leaders."

Skip ahead to 2019, and the media is unabashed carrying water for China and its interests. The United States has the National

Committee to thank for this. As part of its media outreach, the Committee hosted Chinese journalists in the United States in 1974 and worked with the American Society of Newspaper Editors and the major television news networks to arrange trips to China for American journalists. Since that time, media exchanges have included, print, television, and radio reporters from major cities and smaller markets, international and general beats. AOL-Time Warner has also sponsored Chinese journalists from Shanghai and facilitated Chinese internships at *Fortune, Time,* HBO, CNN, Warner Brothers, and "all aspects of the entertainment world,"cxxxiv the same groups that regularly bash Trump over his efforts to put American interests before those of globalists.

The group gushed over China's accession into the World Trade Organization one month after the World Trade Center was struck on September 11, 2001.cxxxv The National Committee's *Annual Report* reported to much fanfare that Chinese exports to the United States had risen 22.4 percent to $125,200,000,000, with exports to China rising 15 percent to $22,000,000,000. "Foreign investors, encouraged by the prospect for China's economy, increased foreign, direct investment to China to $52,700,000,000, causing China for the first time to surpass the United States as the number one destination for FDI," the Committee affirmed.

In 2005, Deputy Secretary of State Robert Zoellick told the National Committee that the U.S.-China relationship was based upon "cooperation as stakeholders...and interests in sustaining political, economic, and security systems that provide common benefits." That year, the group's *Annual Report* was entitled "China's Rise," inspiring Florida Gov. Jeb Bush's "Right to Rise" presidential campaign slogan, based upon elite's preordained conclusion that China had a right to rise on the world stage to overtake the United States as leader of the new world order championed by his father. Elites had expected either Jeb! or Hillary Clinton, the heirs apparent to the White House, to preside over the United States during this transition.

During the second Bush Administration, the American manufacturing base relocated to China. "As the winds of economy change...the importance of China in the global system only increases," the National Committee affirmed in its *2007 Annual Report*. "As China assumes that mantle, we should take pride in the fact that the programs the Committee has conducted over the last 42 years have helped that progress....Exchanges in areas of politics and security... enable policy makers, elected officials, and military leaders from the United States and Greater China to meet and develop working relationships, and discuss sensitive and important issue like Sino-American trade, banking, financial reform, counter terrorism, the environment, food and product safety, space programs...."

The National Committee was positively euphoric over the election of President Barack Obama.cxxxvi on grounds that his "approach to global issues has more in common with China's approach than our current president, (and so) cooperation on the issues is naturally going to become easier."

Entitled "China, U.S., and the Emerging Global Agenda: Focusing on Our Long Term Interests," the Committee praised Microsoft founder Bill Gates for pursuing opportunities in China and Israel for "e-governance" in anticipation of the roll out of Smart cities and Smart government programs.

Liberal billionaire financier and globalist George Soros, who has poured money into the political campaigns of Hillary Clinton, Obama, and other globalist politicians, announced that Communist China should "own" the new world order.

When Obama's Treasury Secretary was asked about Beijing's currency proposal – that of having world trade conducted in renmibi or yuan, instead of the dollar, he said, "We're actually quite open to that."

Christine LaGarde, the head of the International Monetary Fund told reporters, "The way things are going, I wouldn't be surprised if one of these days the IMF had its headquarters in Beijing."

In public appearances, Hillary has described U.S.-China relations as the "new global battle." Yet, privately, in appearances before the Committee as Secretary of State in 2009, she acknowledged that she and Treasury Secretary Tim Geithner "co-led" the effort for the strategic and economic dialog with China. "We believe that these very productive conversations have helped lay the foundation for what both President Obama and President Hu called a positive cooperative and comprehensive U.S.-Chinese relationship for the 21st century."

Treasury Secretary Hank Paulson, who led the U.S. delegation to a U.S.-China Strategic Economic Dialog to facilitate cooperation on investment, energy, and the environment, has also heartily engaged China since presiding over Goldman Sachs.

As dialog was initiated with the Communist Party Secretary

and Vice Premier Wang Yang, Hillary said, "We are enlisting the full range of talent within our government to tackle problems that spill over not just borders and oceans but also traditional bureaucratic boundaries which are sometimes the hardest to overcome...This is ... a culmination of a process that began decades ago when Dr. Kissinger was instrumental in opening the door to the possibility that came to fruition ten years after normalized relations. We were constantly thinking of Henry Kissinger over the last days getting ready for this because his work, his courage, the risks that he took has led us in so many ways to this evening....Since taking this job, I've relied on the wise counsel of many of my predecessors, and Secretary Kissinger has been among the most generous and thoughtful with his guidance and advice."

Among the elites to preside over the National Committee were Carla Hills, who served as U.S. Trade Representative under President George H.W. Bush and as President of the World Bank; Bob McNamara, Secretary of Defense for JKF, and Lee Hamilton, the Vice Chair of the 911 Commission. Its Board Members have included former AIG CEO Maurice "Hank" Greenberg and former Secretary of State Henry Kissinger.

Among its benefactors are those companies which have benefited financially through U.S. engagement with China, including, for example, Time Warner (whose globalist cable news network, CNN, spars with President Donald Trump on a daily basis.), Coca-Cola (now in talks to sell marijuana drinks to dumb down Americans), General Motors (which has received several substantial taxpayer bailouts), British Petroleum (which has polluted America's coastlines with oil spills), HSBC (a global bank which allegedly engages in money laundering for drug cartels; former FBI Director James Comey has served on its Board of Directors, and HSBC donates to the Clinton Foundation), the Department of State (an agency through which Hillary Clinton presided while selling foreign access to public officials in exchange for donations); the Henry Luce Foundation, and the Starr Foundation.

To give an example of how elites are profiting through market access to China, the *Wall Street Journal* reported that the Starr Group, led by Greenberg, has taken control of Dakhong Insurance in a deal described as the first foreign takeover of the state-backed Chinese General Insurance. There are many other deals like this.

By 2018, the National Committee was holding galas for over 400 people, including business leaders, public officials, and senior Chinese diplomats to "reflect on the increasingly complex nature of the bilateral relationship through these challenging and uncertain times." China was identified as the leading threat to the United States, militarily, economically, and strategically. Among the sponsors of the event in which China was identified as the leading threat to the United States militarily, strategically, and economically were the Starr Foundation, Chevron, Ernest & Young, Intel, WalMart; WinXiang, Cisco, Estee Lauder, KPMG, Pfizer, and PayPal.

As criticism mounted and questions were raised about the devastating impact of America's China policy on the United States, the National Committee tried to assuage concerns. While acknowledging that China holds U.S. Treasury notes with reserves approaching $2,500,000,000,000, the National Committee relayed: "Alarmists warn us China has great leverage to harm the United States. Instead of giving China leverage, these enormous reserves pull China and United States more closely together...A prosperous and more fiscally disciplined United States will be able to repay its debt. If China were to dump its United States debt, the American economy would certainly suffer. The value of United States Treasuries would drop and interest rates would rise – but the biggest loser would be China."

Not exactly a vote of confidence. Why should the Americans have to repay the debt run up by corporations and elites who have profited at the expense of ordinary citizens? Elites drove these disastrous policies to enrich themselves. Why should the people bear the consequences? Americans weren't consulted on the matter nor was the elite's China policy put to a vote. The media was even co-opted, preventing an honest discussion about China. In fact, those who challenged the elite narrative were viciously attacked, silenced, and defamed. Americans were told to tighten their belts. At the same time, elites have eliminated the means through which the country can truly become prosperous again by running up the debt, flooding the country with economic refugees, relocating jobs overseas, driving taxes through the roof, preventing the country from becoming energy independent, and then locking the country into a series of interdependencies that prevent the country from being able to act in its own interests.

"Dr. Kissinger led us here," the National Committee conceded in a report, dated August of 2009. "When President Carter established diplomatic relations with China, leadership prevailed. (We were) stunned by the vehemence of the criticism against President Carter, National Security Advisor Brzezinski, Secretary Vance, and many others, even though their decisions were clearly in the national interest. But thanks to President Nixon and Secretary Kissinger and President Carter and Dr. Brzezinski, we have succeeded in our task."[cxxxvii] Were those decisions "clearly in the national interest?" Were they even intended to be? Such is the double talk of globalists.

This was just one flank of the journey, which was enjoined by Russia, Israel, and China leading to the Belt and Road Initiative, a multi-trillion dollar investment boondoggle. The once great United States where anyone with enough drive, talent, and initiative could achieve the American dream was in the scopes of the globalists who sought to kill the goose that laid the golden egg and replace it with a golden calf.

Nearly a century earlier, aspiring monopolists working hand-in-hand with international bankers and the British Crown announced "our plan" to pursue a national industrial policy for private gain and to eliminate competition while shoring up the world's wealth and resources into the hands of a few. In the decades that followed, they would plunder the American treasury, strip the country of its resources, steal the jobs of its citizens, and make starting a new business virtually impossible for ordinary people, transforming the glittering city on a hill into a desert with a view to building a communist world order that they would lead and control. What these elites wanted was privilege, the privilege to look down on humanity from the depths of hell.

Laying in their wake were mountains of debt and suffering inflicted upon innocent people whom they had betrayed and deceived and whose country they had sullied, destabilized, and corrupted beyond recognition. Wrestling power from their hands to restore the country for, by, and of the people, was at the core of Donald Trump's campaign promise of Making American Great Again; it was a platform the globalists rightly feared as it marked the end of their tyrannical and exploitative reign over humanity.

VI.
The Shadow Dragon

After President Barack Obama secured a second term in office, the globalists launched their end game – a multi-trillion dollar investment project through China called the Belt and Road Initiativecxxxviii which was to build infrastructure and develop and connect Europe, Asia, Africa, Oceania -- and eventually Latin America, through road, rail, and sea routes, with a view to extending its influence. Russia and China launched a side project, the Ice Silk Road, to develop the Arctic region to extract oil and gas and collaborate on infrastructure, development, and technological projects.

Since the power of China was consolidated within the Communist Party, as opposed to the people – just as the globalists had designed it to be – China could impose policies and invest money without having to put the matter before public debate or concern itself with public deception. Should the people dare rebel, they could expect to be ruthlessly suppressed by the Butchers of Beijing. Among the China apologists was *New York Times* contributor Thomas Friedman, the son-in-law of billionaire real estate developer Matthew Bucksbaum. cxxxix"One party autocracy ...can just impose politically difficult, but critically important policies needed, to move a society forward in the 21st century," said the Oxford-educated Friedman.

The globalists were ready to align themselves with a communist government that advocates "cleansing" the North American continent with nuclear and chemical weapons, harvests the organs of its dissidents, and engages in rapacious debt diplomacy throughout the world.

Obama may have been alluding to the elites when he announced to much public derision, "If you've been successful, you didn't get there on your own......I'm always struck by people who say 'It's gotta be that I was just so smart.' There are a lot of smart people out there. 'It must be because I worked harder than everyone else.' Let me tell you something, there are a whole bunch of hard working people out there. If you were successful, someone along the line gave you some help.... Somebody helped to create this unbelievable American system that we have that allowed you to thrive. Somebody invested in roads and bridges. If you got a business, you didn't build that. Somebody else made that happen.... The Internet didn't get there on its own."

The elites had rigged the system, bribed public officials, received taxpayer-supported R&D to make products sold to markets forged by the federal government, enabling them to make the profits while the taxpayers foot the bill. In many cases, for all their braggadocio about their success, privilege, and innovation, elites were frequently entitled beneficiaries of a corrupt system that was rigged against meritocracy and designed to reinforce their privilege.

They didn't have to take risks as they always had a safety net to fall back on. If they became overextended or victims of their own failed practices, they could expect to be bailed out, ensuring that they won even when they lost.

In contrast, if average citizen were to fail at an enterprise of his own making, he risked losing his home, his pension, and the financial wherewithal to send his children to college. He most likely would not get bailed out by the banks. Instead, his credit might be so shaken, that they might not qualify for a loan for a long time, and even then, would likely to be subjected to an extraordinarily high interest rate.

Worse, as a little fish in a big pond, he was forced to compete in markets that major corporations had rigged to their advantage while he supported the corporations with his taxes as they evaded their own.

For all the money the American public has invested in so-called infrastructure projects, there should not be a single pot hole or crumbling bridge anywhere in sight, but the country is riddled with them while the elites fly around in their expensive jets and opulent, multi-million dollar houses advocating more taxes so that the people can pay their fair share of the national debt that has exploded, making the rich even richer. The American people are crying foul.

At least sixty countries were included along the Belt and Road Initiative, a plan anticipated to cost anywhere from $4,000,000,000,000 to $8,000,000,000,000. The Asian Infrastructure Investment Bank would finance the loans in lieu of the Western-controlled World Bank and IMF, realigning the world order under China's control, with the corporations profiting even more through this realignment. International commerce was to be transaction in the renminbi as opposed to the dollar, with the renminbi tossed into the "basket of currencies" one month before the Secretary of State Hillary Clinton was projected to win the 2016 presidential election.

While the globalists mock America's quaint Christian values, can anyone truly say that China's frightful dishonesty, lack of concern for human rights, theft of intellectual property, pathological greed and power lust, professions of racial superiority are superior? Would anyone prefer a world led by China over one led by the noble United States, which until its infestation and corruption at the hands of unprincipled, rapacious elites, was a magnet for the people throughout the world who sought to pursue the American dream and embrace its values?

When Chinese President Xi Jinping addressed the Belt and Road Forum in 2017, he laid out five goals: 1.) to coordinate policy among participating nations[cxl]; 2.) to connect facilities and utilities as reflected in the New Eurasian Continental Bridge, the China-Mongolia Russian Economic Corridor, and the China-Pakistan Economic Corridor; 3.) to secure unimpeded trade; [cxli]4.) to tap global financial institutions, like the Asian Infrastructure Bank, the Silk Road Fund, the New Development Bank to invest billions of dollars in projects, generating new markets, contracts, and opportunities for corporations with public funds and through debt diplomacy; and 5.) to forge transnational relationships to increase cooperation in the areas of science, education, and health through scholarships and other means.

Xi announced $14,500,000,000 in Silk and Road funding and lending schemes for China's Development Bank and Export-Import Bank of China worth $36,000,000,000 and $19,000,000,000 respectively. He called on the global financial community to establish a BRI fund worth $43,000,000,000.

That year, Fitch ratings, one of the big three credit rating agencies, advised that BRI's infrastructure projects were driven by politics, rather than commercial needs, resulting in substantial risks for banks financing them. The sovereign debt of 25 BRI nations is regarded as junk by the three main ratings agencies and therefore the banks would be assuming debt on underperforming assets, potentially resulting in loan defaults. If the countries that borrow money to invest in BRI projects default on their loans, elites would be able to buy up their assets for pennies on the dollar.

A number of Western corporations are lining up to take advantage of the opportunities on offer, like including, for example, Honeywell, Siemens, and Citibank. General Electric has reportedly acquired business in China valued at $2,300,000,000 in 2016, a jump from a reported $400,000,000 in 2014. DuPont, Ford, General

Motors, IBM, Microsoft, Motorola, and a number of other multinationals have also made significant inroads into the Chinese market.

Among the countries involved in the Belt and Road projects include Israel, Saudi Arabia, China, Russia, Australia, Argentina, Brazil, and Peru, among others stretching through Europe, Africa, the former Soviet Union, the Middle East, Eurasia, Latin America, and Oceania, accounting for what is approaching nearly three-quarters of the world's population.

In 2013, China established an Asia Infrastructure Bank, whose founding members include the United Kingdom, Israel, India, Russia, Germany, South Korea, France, South Africa, China, and dozens of other countries.cxlii According to a report prepared for the 2016 Annual Meeting of the Asian Development Bank, investment and planning in ongoing Belt and Road projects will reach as high as $240,000,000,000, with total investment needs in Asia expected to be larger than that. Some estimate that as much as $3,600,000,000,000 is needed to develop South Asia to meet the growing needs of its population and trend toward urbanization, projects that will be fulfilled through public-private partnerships. President Xi is looking towards the "natural extension" of BRI into Latin America.cxliii

In 2013, the year BRI was launched, RILIN Enterprises, a privately held Chinese construction and trade conglomerate pledged $2,000,000 to the Clinton Foundation and $120,000 to Clinton strategist Terry McAuliffe's gubernatorial campaign.cxliv According to its promotional literature, China RILIN oversees "a full range of enterprises across the globe," including infrastructure projects, logistics, construction, and port operations." The group is affiliated with the West Corporation and directed by industrialist Wenliang Wang, who established the Embassy of China in Washington, DC and U.S.-China cultural exchange programs through Harvard University and other universities.

The global institutions were on board with the envisioned global debt project. Former World Bank President Jim Yong Kim said that the World Bank is "well positioned" to Support BRI.cxlv The United Nations Development Programme has partnered with people "of all levels of society to help build nations that can withstand crisis and drive and sustain the kind of growth that improves the quality of life for everyone."

In September of 2016, the UNDP and Communist China signed a Memorandum of Understanding in which the China Development Bank was designated to help distribute wealth globally from the "haves" to the "have nots" in the interests of "sustainable development." That year, China's Communist Party incorporated the Belt and Road Initiative into its platform, reflecting China's efforts to expand its hegemony throughout the world. The Communist Party demanded $8,000,000,000,000 to develop projects linking Europe, Africa, and Asia. While President Xi has characterized the Belt and Road Initiative as "the project of the century," the *Financial Times* ponders whether it might "export the worst aspects of the Chinese economy while increasing the strains on its already stressed financial system."[cxlvi]

Through its "Made in China 2025" initiative, the Chinese Communist Party has rolled out a Smart Cities program while taking steps to control 90 percent of the world's high tech industry including robotics, biotechnology and Artificial Intelligence.

The RWR's *Belt and Road Monitoring* has documented China's lucrative deals throughout the world. To cite one example, Saudi Arabia's Ministry of Housing and National Housing Company signed a $2,700,000,000 agreement with PowerChina International to construct a 17,000 unit Al Asfar residential complex.

Maritime facilities for the King Salmon International Complex for Maritime Industries and Services received $3,000,000,000 for engineering work, the construction of shipyards, and offshore drilling projects. Saudi Arabia is now on track to become a global ship builder through an International Maritime Industries joint venture with Armaco.

The Ministry of Housing and Real Estate Development Fund signed a $1,200,000,000 agreement with Sany-Alameriah, a Saudi-Chinese joint venture, to build the Telal Alghoroob housing project with 9,500 units in Dammam and Jeddah.

The United Arab Emirates-based China Arab TV signed a strategic agreement with Hunan Broadcasting System's Mango TV to broadcast Chinese culture in all 22 Arab League countries from its station in Dubai.

The Ethiopian Road Authority signed five road construction contracts with Chinese companies, valued at $305,000,000.[cxlvii] Rwanda signed three Memoranda of Understanding (MOUs) with

Alibaba Group to establish an electronic world trade platform (eWTP) hub in Rwanda.

Reflecting growing cooperation between the two countries, Russia and China signed nine cooperation agreements in areas that include healthcare, tourism, education, and media during the 19th session of the China-Russia Committee on Humanities Cooperation. Russia's Ministry of Health and China's Ministry of Health separately agreed to research exchanges, coordinating the regulation of medical drugs and devices, and conduct joint medical response drills.[cxlviii]

Israel, America's number one ally and aid recipient, has allowed China to operate Haifa port, near Israel's alleged nuclear-armed submarines, with the concomitant risk that the Communist regime could spy on visiting U.S. Navy ships.[cxlix] As *The Asia Times* reported,[cl] "Two multi-billion dollar Chinese seaports near critical Israeli sites are raising concerns over potential security issues ... with Washington. China is constructing seaports at two sites where the U.S. 6th Fleet deploys, in Haifa next to Israel's main naval base and Ashdod near Tel Aviv, prompting concerns about China's military potential in the Mediterranean Sea and Middle East." *Haaretz* reported that "No one in Israel thought about the strategic ramifications." Elliot Abrams, a neoconservative with the Council of Foreign Relations, wrote that Israelis have also raised questions over the security implications of China's investment in Israeli infrastructure projects through the Belt and Road initiative. Even neoconservative hawk and Israeli first National Security Adviser John Bolton has sought to rein in the Israel-China relationship, *Haaretz* reported.[cli]

As of 2016, China's direct investment to Israel was $16,000,000,000 while China was projected to overtake the United States as the leading source of overseas investment in Israel, which has traded its technology for access to China's vast markets.[clii]

By the end of 2017, the bilateral trade volume between China and Israel was reportedly $13,000,000,000 with Chinese companies investing in Israeli medical services, clean technology, and other sectors.

Israel is a recipient of billions of dollars of support and protection from the United States, which has intervened in the Middle East for its defense, often at the cost of U.S. blood and treasure. At the same time, Israel has emerged as a key strategic partner for China, which is posing a threat to the United States.

The China-Israeli relationship gradually took shape after the World Wars. For example, Saul Eisenberg, a Jewish billionaire who fled Europe during the Holocaust, immigrated to Shanghai, where he used his contacts to market Israeli weaponry in Israel, often returning to the Jewish state with a "shopping list" that included missiles, radar, artillery shell, and armor.[cliii] China and Israel "did not have diplomatic ties," *Newsweek* reported. "If word got out, Israel knew that the Americans would be furious."[cliv]

The Chinese "did not want to aggravate their traditional allies, the Soviet Union and the Arab bloc – by doing business with Israel," *Newsweek* reported. China is now Israel's leading trade partner in Asia.

Through the channels that were created after World War II, Israel and China have forged many lucrative deals. The China Development Bank and Israel investment company, Clal Industries have provided funding for the Infinity Group, an Israeli-Chinese equity fund worth more than $1,500,000,000. "An Israeli ecosystem must be created in China," Amir Gal-Or, the founder of Infinity Group told reporters. "If each Israeli company will work here alone, it will not last." Clal Industries is one of Israel's leading investment companies, one that owns a portfolio of investments ranging from heavy industry, biotechnology, hi-tech, and energy companies.

The Gatehub Sino-Israel Business and Innovation Center has brought together senior governmental and municipal officials, tech and business leaders, technology companies, private equity and venture capital funds, private investors, among others from China and Israel to link a "chain of cross-border centers and a network of Chinese and Israeli tech and business experts to collaborate on projects, investments, mergers and acquisitions, and technology transfers, matching capital with projects. Israeli and Chinese ministers have signed 10 bilateral agreements in health, science, education, environmental protection, and other areas. "We want to marry our technology with China's capacity," Israeli Prime Minister Bibi Netanyahu told his audience there. "We in Israel are eager to share with China our science and technology that can better the lives of all mankind, and the people of China" Netanyahu reached out to Beijing to establish an Israeli-China free trade agreement.

Yet Israel and China's rise has come at the expense of the United States. As Vice President Mike Pence said, "To win the commanding heights of the 21st century economy, Beijing has directed its bureaucracies and businesses to obtain American intellectual property, the foundation of our economic leadership, by any means necessary." *Haaretz* also observed that "Israel will have to choose between America and China."[clv]

In order to facilitate ties and understanding, the *Times of Israel*[clvi] reported, a group of Israelis living in Beijing have dedicated themselves to spreading Jewish culture and wisdom in China. The Chinese have volunteered to translate articles and books about Judaism into Chinese. *Newsweek* reported that the Chinese are looking to the *Talmud* for business advice.[clvii]

Among the American Jews living in China who helped open China's markets to the West was Sidney Rittenberg, a journalist and member of the Chinese Communist Party who had applied to work for the OSS and who knew Mao Zedong personally. As a result of his personal connections, Rittenberg launched a consulting practice representing some of the largest brands, including Levis Strauss, Microsoft, and Hughes Aircraft, all of which have tapped into the Chinese markets. After World War II, Rittenberg remained in China to assist with the UN famine relief program. In this role he interpreted messages from Chairman Mao, who reportedly affirmed that he wanted to maintain a constructive relationship with the United States to rebuild his country since he did not want to deal with the Soviets. Today, China, Israel, and Russia have linked together to realign power in the world away from the United States and toward themselves.

Netanyahu has even hosted China's Vice President Wang Qishan and with Jack Ma, the CEO and founder of the e-commerce site Alibaba, in Jerusalem. He affirmed that the meeting "reflects the growing ties between our countries, our economies, our peoples."

The consequences for the United States have been devastating. In November of 2018, the National Defense Strategic Commission reported that "The security and well being of the United States are at the greatest risk today than at any time in decades. America's military superiority has eroded to a dangerous degree....Rivals and adversaries are challenging the United States on many fronts and in many domains. America's ability to defend its allies, its partners, and its own vital interests is increasingly in doubt. If the nation does not act promptly to remedy these circumstances, the consequences will be grave....The U.S. military could suffer unacceptably high casualties and the loss of major capital assets in its next conflict. It might struggle to win or perhaps lose a war against China and Russia. The United States is particularly at risk at being overwhelmed should its military be forced to fight on two or more fronts simultaneously...."

In another report – this one released by the Pentagon in January, 2019, [clviii] the Defense Intelligence Agency argued that China's strategy of "acquiring technology by any means necessary," which includes requiring companies to divulge trade secrets before they were allowed to tap into China's markets has ensured that China is now "on the verge of fielding some of the most modern weapons systems in the world," which, in turn will "enable (it) to impose its will in the region." China already has the capability to launch weapons that could reach parts of the United States, including Alaska and Hawaii.[clix]

Google, Yahoo, and Microsoft all made Faustian bargains with China in order to gain access to those lucrative markets. They have censored and manipulated results in their search engines, and in the case of Yahoo, have identified the authors of Internet content that the Chinese government had found objectionable, resulting in the imprisonment of at least one dissident.

Tech companies have also censored Americans by silencing and de-platforming those who challenge globalist narratives and agendas, preventing them from reaching audience through social media. Worrying, China has issued a "social credit score" to its citizens which can cut off those who score poorly to public transportation and any other service managed and controlled by technology, which is being used against people rather than in service of them. Already Americans are finding themselves at the mercy of technology as their private information is sold into the dark web, their emails are hacked, their energy grids rendered vulnerable, their meta data harvested and sold to market products and services to them, and so on. The Internet, which held out the promise to connect the world and facilitate the exchange of information has been rendered dark.

Two Chinese backers allegedly infiltrated 45 U.S. tech companies and government agencies, including the US Navy, according to a 2018 Department of Justice indictment. China's Ministry of State Security was similarly accused to infiltrating IBM and HP Enterprise, using their systems to gain access to systems belonging to their government and military clients.[clx]

While the American dream was being crushed within the

United States, Chinese President Xi was unveiling the "China Dream," to pursue a "great renewal of the Chinese nation" within an international system that stood to offer an alternative political model to the Western one. Media personalities, sports figures, national leaders, and so-called celebrities of one sort or another quixotically cheered the demise of America and mocked the American people while doing their utmost to pit the American people against each other to distract, demoralize, and disempower them, just as the Communists had done in China.

VII.
The Conquest of America

Among the greatest obstacles to a new world order led by China is Christianity. Within atheist China, Christianity has been outlawed. As China's money flows into the United States, efforts have been made to extinguish Christianity here as well.

Remarkably, schools are being told they can't distribute candy canes during Christmas on grounds that the J shape of the candy cane symbolizes Jesus and therefore violates the establishment clause and offends new arrivals to the United States.clxi

Wishing neighbors "Merry Christmas" can now be considered hate speech while depicting ghoulish pagan murders and blood sacrifices on Halloween is considered acceptable.

Posters that include the word "Christmas" have been banned from schools while beautiful, inspiring Christmas songs like "Joy to the World" and "Silent Night" have been silenced.

A teacher in Texas who decorated her classroom with a scene from Charles Schulz's Christmas classic, "A Charlie Brown Christmas," was forced to remove a replica of the iconic feeble Christmas tree to spare feelings.

Students sending seasonal cards to soldiers were told to make "holiday cards" so as not to offend anyone.

Similarly, Christmas trees, wreaths, and even the colors red and green have been curtailed during the Christmas season as part of a coordinated effort to avoid any reference to Christianity, Christ, or God and demoralize Christians.

On a fundamental level, attacks on Christianity are nothing new. The *Bible* warns Christians about the persecution people of faith endure, accounting, in part, for the decision of the nation's founders to include an establishment clause within the Constitution, to prevent the government from restricting the expression of religion or discriminating against those who practice it. Christianity is a beautiful religion that encourages its adherents to cultivate a personal relationship with God and look inward, upwards, and to one's parents, inner voice, conscience, and to the *Bible* itself for moral guidance instead of the state. Christianity brings out the best in its followers, inspiring their compassion, charity, and tolerance.

The positive contributions Christianity has made towards

American society and its institutions would require a book in and of itself. Suffice to say, contrary to what the globalists suggest, Christianity is not a hindrance to progress; it has elevated mankind in remarkable ways.

Christianity informed the nation's founders to enshrine freedoms and values within the nation's founding documents that enabled the United States to transcend the old world to create a world anew.

As Pope Benedict XCI beautifully remarked on the South Lawn of the White House in 2008, "From the dawn of the Republic, America's quest for freedom has been guided by the conviction that the principles governing political and social life are intimately linked to a moral order based on the dominion of God the Creator. The framers of this nation's founding documents drew upon this conviction when they proclaimed the 'self-evident truth' that all men are created equal and endowed with inalienable rights grounded in the laws of nature and of nature's God. The course of American history demonstrates the difficulties, the struggles, and the great intellectual and moral resolve which were demanded to shape a society which faithfully embodied these noble principles. In that process, which forged the soul of the nation, religious beliefs were a constant inspiration and driving force as, for example, in the struggle against slavery and in the Civil Rights Movement. In our time too, particularly in moments of crisis, Americans continue to find their strength in a commitment to this patrimony of shared ideals and aspirations."

Similarly, the 19th century French diplomat and historian Alexis de Tocqueville wrote, "I went into the churches of America and heard her pulpits aflame with righteousness. (Only then) did I understand the secret of her genius and power. America is great because she is good, and if America ever ceases to be good, she will cease to be great."clxii

Making America great again was never about returning to slavery or embracing white supremacy. The faith of the American people led them to free the slaves after the old world enslaved them. The East India Company promoted the slave trade prior to Americans spilling their own blood to discontinue the horrid practice.

Remarkably, globalists have shifted the blame of slavery away from themselves and onto the good American people, who not only did not want to enslave others, but didn't want to be enslaved themselves. Nor were they racists. The America of old believed in equal treatment before the law and under God, not preferential treatment for the powerful. They believed that all people are endowed by their Creator with equal rights, not the Orwellian view that some are more equal than others. They stood shoulder-to-shoulder with Civil Rights leader Martin Luther King, Jr., who envisioned a dream in which people would be judged not by the color of their skin but by the content of their character, a character refined by religion and made pleasing to their Creator. Christians risked their lives to protect Jews during the Holocaust and coordinated the underground railroads. They were at the core of making America good. They believed in freedom.

While old world materialists have condemned Christians as backwards, their faith has inspired great works of literature, magnificent art, groundbreaking science, and a system of government that ingeniously checks abuses of power and protects the rights of the minorities. Christians elevated the status of women, children, and the vulnerable while reinforcing a strong family unit, the fundamental building block for a stable, well functioning society. Far from persecuting those who fell short of the glory of God, their religion encouraged them to love the sinner, even if they hated the sin. The faith has elevated mankind and soothed the souls of the suffering. Christianity is at the heart and soul of the American experience.

Secretary of State, Henry Kissinger, who was himself a foreign transplant, appreciated that America's greatness had been achieved through the values of its people and therefore sought to undermine those values to weaken American resolve. He was a materialist and globalist who believed that private interests trump values and that God should be consigned to the dustbin of history.

In its quest for easy money and lucrative government contracts, the American political establishment, that grew corrupt through entangled foreign alliances, propped up countries like Saudi Arabia and Communist China that have threatened its own interests. As Saudi and Chinese money poured into the American political system and offered the prospect of lucrative deals and government contracts, the corporate and political classes readily accommodated their interests and values for short term gain. Christianity is now under assault from all directions.

On the campaign trail, Donald Trump promised to put America

first, throwing the elites into a fit of apoplexy. The opposition against him was real. For the first time in a long while, the American people had a leader strong and principled enough to fight for the country, shrewd and experienced enough to understand the issues at hand, and enough of a maverick not to cave. His challenger, Hillary Clinton, had rigged the primaries against her leading challenger Bernie Sanders, secured questions in advance of debates, and enjoyed almost universal support among globalists, who controlled all the levers of power, and yet, miraculously Trump won, sending elites into conniptions.

This is not to say that Trump deserves a free pass, however.

Americans must remain vigilant and demand accountability from their elected officials.

Trump's message struck a chord with the American people.

He drew large crowds over his promise to "build a wall" and instate immigration controls. The globalists quickly jumped upon his anti-immigrant rhetoric to characterize the candidate and his followers as racist, even though African Americans, Latin Americans, and people of every race, color, and creed were embraced by the American First movement and enjoyed higher levels of employment and opportunities under his leadership. What the elites tried to portray as the struggle of a dying, reactionary, privileged white America against everyone else was actually that of a genuine, grassroots uprising of the American people against the corrupt, unaccountable, parasitic elites.

When Christian Americans traversed the globe, they shared the Gospel, medicines, education to enlighten and elevate the people around the world. They valued diversity as an expression of God's creativity, sought to preserve the cultures in which they came into contact, and championed the uniqueness and talents of others. They were stewards of the world who lived to serve and help others.

In contrast, elites introduced drugs, gambling, and dependency into Indian Country and the world to enrich themselves further when they were not otherwise flooding Indians tribes with non-Natives, seizing control of their governments, plundering their resources, and mocking their cultures. Elites introduced opium to China and squashed the traditions and spirituality of the Chinese to weaken and demoralize them. They have flooded Europe with refugees who cannot and will not assimilate and who are tapping out entitlement programs reserved for the citizens. They armed Mexican gangs with guns and plied them with drugs. They thrust Venezuela into despair and destitution. They routinely mock Christianity and Judaism to demoralize their adherents. They pit people against each other, men against women, white against black, Christian against Muslim, Muslim against Jew, the poor against the rich, the old against the young, all the while accusing everyone else of being unspeakably bigoted. Communist literature has encouraged division and civil strife to weaken nations and destroy them from within. The people have had enough. With the election of Donald Trump, God gave the American people a period of grace. Will they choose the high or the low road? Will they find the strength within to rid themselves of the globalist cancer?

In generations past, Americans considered it a disgrace to accept welfare and a privilege to work to support themselves and their families. Recent immigrants from the poorest of countries considered it a privilege to live in a free country like the United States, one that offered them the opportunity to make something of themselves through dint of hard work. Even if they might not realize the American dream during their life time, they sought to build a foundation upon which their children could have a better life, with each generation emerging more prosperous than the last. Society was fluid, with people able to rise and fall within the classes through their own initiative or lack thereof. Even if they might try and fail, they could persevere and try again. In contrast, European social democracy ensured one's destiny at birth. The rich would always be rich and would have the tools and contacts to become richer still. The middle class would never rise above their station, and the poor languished in misery throughout their lives.

The American government now fosters dependency, with the elite catapulting the world's poor to America's door. Initially entitlements were promoted as a means through which corporations could improve shareholder value. Entitlement spending has since became a cottage industry. Immigration has been weaponized to make way for a new world order. Globalists funded the La RAZA Movement that actively recruited and promoted Mexican immigrants to agitate for globalism by claiming that America should be conquered by Mexico through immigration as punishment for having "stolen" Mexican land centuries ago.

While globalists have challenged Trump's efforts to build a wall between the United States and Mexico, the Vatican, British

Royalty, Israel, and elites of every distinction, have built walls around their territories to protect themselves from those who wish them harm. Even China erected the Great Wall to ward off invasions and raids from Eurasian nomads.

Americans resent having to pay higher medical insurance premiums while illegal immigrants get free medical care, and veterans languish on the streets without support. Ordinary American citizens realistically fear succumbing to homelessness as they struggle to make ends meet and watch their taxes grow to support Section 8 housing along with free education, food stamps, and an assortment of other benefits for illegal immigrants and economic refugees.

Globalists respond to the concerns of ordinary citizens by mocking them and cheering their demise, actually providing timelines in the news of years in which the United States can expect white Christian Americans to die off and become minorities in their own country. They celebrate diversity by mixing people of different cultures together and then pitting them against each other.

While disastrous globalist policies and war have destabilized the societies from which many immigrants have fled, mass migration is part of a larger globalist agenda. Consider, if you will, that in 2018, leaders from the Vatican and World Council of Churches convened in Geneva and Rome to combat "xenophobia, racism, populism and nationalism within the context of migration" on grounds that migration is "an inherent feature of the human condition" and that populist nationalism a "political strategy (that promotes) fears of individual groups in order to assert the need for an authoritarian political power to protect the interests of the dominant social and ethnic group established in particular territory." Refusing refugees and migrants was "contrary to the example and calling of Jesus Christ," its report suggested in an effort to shame Christian countries into accepting more immigrants even though globalists routinely reject and mock God. While wrapping themselves around the cross, the WCC and Vatican appealed to United Nations to "end intolerance against all migrants." The West "has a moral responsibility" to welcome immigrants, the Pope said while refusing to share the Vatican's gold with the poor or house fleeing migrants within its own gated community.

Moving in lock step with the globalist agenda, the mainstream media has accused Americans of being racist, feeble minded, reactionary xenophobes, actually mocking and disparaging them for not going along with the program.

Yet it is clear that another agenda is at play. Not only do Communists advocate a strategy of overwhelming the United States with immigrants, but globalist groups have organized caravans from the United States and Mexico, like *Pueblos sin Fronteras,* which have called for open borders.

Another tell is that the Chair Emeritus of the International Rescue Committee, an organization which champions asylum seekers, is none other than Winston Lord, a Yale graduate and member of Skull and Bones. In addition to attending meetings with President Richard Nixon, Secretary of State Henry Kissinger, and Communist Chinese Chairman Mao Zedong, Lord accompanied Nixon on his historic trip to China and served as U.S. Ambassador to China under President George H.W. Bush.

The IRC was subsidized by the National War Fund whose president was Winston Aldrich, an American financier and scion of a prominent political family who served as U.S. Ambassador to the United Kingdom. Married to a Rockefeller, Aldrich became President and Chairman of Chase National Bank which coordinated financial assistance for the UK and Europe after World War II. Parroting globalist talking points, the IRC opines: "Central Americans fleeing violence and persecution have the right to apply for protection, A new U.S. policy that will push these desperate asylum seekers back into Mexico is not only cruel but illegal." Among the IRC's champions is actress Meryl Streep who endorsed Hillary Clinton for President and then promptly joined the "Resistance" after Trump won in her place.

The International Rescue Committee, which established 191 field offices in over 30 crisis torn communities to help refugees survive conflict and rebuild countries after wars, is presided over not by an American – but a Brit – UK Foreign Secretary David Milliband to be exact.

Founded during World War II, the IRC was established to help Jews flee Nazi Germany. After the IRC facilitated the emigration of European Jews to Israel, China, and the United States, the group expanded its mandate to include other types of refugees. The IRC's antecedent, the International Relief Association, was founded in Germany by communists, some of whom survived Stalin's purges in Russia and who were members of the Socialist Workers Party. Among those purged was Jay Lovestone, the head of the Communist Party of

America who worked with intelligence agencies to establish escape routes for refugees during the World Wars. After 1942, the group morphed into the IRC. Anyone who believes that these people are genuinely concerned with human rights need only consider the millions of people who have lost their lives and been persecuted under communist rule and who have perished through forced migration efforts.

Arising from the ashes of the OSS, the intelligence community has worked hand-in-hand with the media and Hollywood to shape public opinion. The National Committee of U.S.-China Relations has admittedly cultivated key figures within academia to advance the globalist agenda. Hollywood and Big Media were all too happy to oblige with the promise of tapping the lucrative Chinese markets. To cite an example, the Associated Press and Communist Chinese-controlled *Xinhua* have affirmed that "the two news agencies have broad cooperation in areas including new media, application of artificial intelligence (AI), and economic information."[clxiii] While Trump has taken CNN to task for reporting "fake news," Mei Yan,[clxiv] the daughter of a Mao Zedong's propagandist, has worked as an executive at CNN, News Corp., and Viacom where she was managing director of MTV Greater China and chief representative of Viacom Asia.[clxv]

Elite actors, journalists, and film directors whose employers are seeking access into China's lucrative markets, have used their platforms to promote globalist political candidates while attacking nationalists like Trump. Dare they challenge the status quo, theses spokesmen for the globalist cause quickly find themselves out of a job. The American people have responded by turning off the TV, abandoning movie theaters, and withdrawing their support from so-called celebrities who are increasingly perceived as propagandists who owe their position less to talent than their willingness to advance political views that do not serve the public's interest.

Hillary Clinton has long enjoyed cozy ties with Hollywood, transforming the movie industry into a fundraising machine for her wider political ambitions when she is not otherwise engaged in vacuous, and at times, cringe-worthy celebrity appearances and photo-ops with so-called teen idols. Can anyone truly believe that a serious leader and policy expert would hang out with reality TV stars and pop idols. Where does she find the time? Success within Hollywood is often contingent upon good marketing, the right connections, rather than talent, reflecting a rigged system. If sparkling unicorn excrement can become a trend among young girls today, following the profitability of the pet rock of yesteryear, then anything or anyone can acquire fame with the right amount of publicity, a field in which Hollywood excels. Their latest product is globalism.

Americans can long nostalgically for the days of lore when Hollywood produced family-friendly films with well written scripts, carefully executed plots, and actors with enviable good looks, admirable character, and charisma. The Golden Age of Hollywood produced movies that moved, inspired, educated and celebrated the American dream, its people, and its values. Now, aside from showcasing the latest technology possessed by elites, movies and celebrities are decidedly anti-American. Hollywood promoted a shameless tongue-thrusting, naked former teen idol Miley Cyrus swinging on a wrecking ball as if to symbolize the controlled demolition of the United States. Comedian Kathy Griffin made an appearance with what appeared to be Trump's severed bloody head in the tradition of a terrorist flaunting an American trophy kill. Talented actor Robert DeNiro ranted like a madman about Trump, calling him a "mutt, punk, dog, pig, and con" for interfering with Hollywood's marketing opportunities in China. Celebrities have used their platforms to tear down the country, stir up racial divisions, and attack prominent conservatives, all in the name of love and bringing the country together. Their desperate behavior has created a sort of cognitive dissonance that has led Americans to wonder whose interests they are really serving. Hollywood has flooded the country with dross while NFL players "take a knee" against the American flag and patriotism. So-called celebrities act as if they are taking marching orders from Communist China. In many cases, they are.

China increasingly controls Hollywood and the NFL through money and marketing opportunities. In order to get access to Chinese markets, the Chinese Communist Party is permitted to weigh in on movie scripts, accounting for the anti-Americans and anti-Trump messaging that many actors and movies now espouse.clxvi When China took exception to the depiction of Chinese villains in *Red Dawn*, MGM responded by digitally erasing the Chinese troops and replacing them with North Koreans.

China's influence on Sony executives led the creators of *Pixels* to depict aliens blasting a hole through the Taj Mahal instead of the Great Wall of China. "China wields enormous influence over how it is depicted in the movies Americans make and watch," the Central Tibetan Administration observed. "It's part of a broader push by the government to take control of its global narrative and present a friendlier, less menacing image of China to the world."[clxvii] China owes its influence in Hollywood to its "inexhaustible cash reserves" as the movie industry faces declining revenue due to competition from Amazon, Netflix, and YouTube along with high ticket prices at theaters at a time when people have less disposable income and movies offer mediocre, anti-American, uninspiring, dumbed down content.

In an effort to make up budget shortfalls, Hollywood moguls and directors have become afraid of offending the Chinese government. As of a few decades ago, Hollywood was critical of China, with the *Seven Years of Tibet* accurately portraying the brutal Chinese treatment of Tibetans. Martin Scorsese's *Kundun* overrode objections from Chinese officials to portray the Dalai Lama as a sympathetic figure. Now "there is a notion that its propaganda has not worked well enough, so this is where the film industry comes in," the Asia Society opined. "There's a real sensitivity to the blockbuster power of Hollywood."[clxviii] China has bankrolled a growing number of top-tier films. China helped finance 12 of the top 100 highest-grossing films from 1997 to 2013. In the five years that followed, China co-financed 41 top-grossing Hollywood films, with financially-strapped. Desperate to tap China's fast-growing box office market, Hollywood studios readily concede to China's demands. "We have a huge market, and we want to share it with you," Zhang Xun, the president of the state-owned production company told film directors, but that access comes with strings. "We want films that are heavily invested in Chinese culture, not one or two shots," she said. "We want to see positive Chinese images."clxix

China has also attempted to control film distribution channels. For example, Wang Jianlin, China's second richest man, doubled his stake in AMC Entertainment Holdings, Inc. (AMC) within 18 months. Sony Pictures Entertainment formed an alliance with Dalian Wanda, one of the world's largest Chinese media empires. "The Chinese government and its support of censorship now have a surprisingly big hand in shaping the movies that Americans make and watch," the *Washington Post* reported.[clxx] Films like *Transformers IV, X-Men:*

Days of Future Past, Looper, Gravity, and *Iron Man 3* have conformed their scripts to accommodate Chinese censors and audiences. "The reasons are obvious: There is a ton of money at stake."

Walt Disney Studios signed an agreement in 2014 with Shanghai Media Group Pictures to develop Disney-branded movies while American and Chinese writers have partnered with filmmakers to develop stories that draw upon Chinese themes.[clxxi]

Johnny Depp made his first trip to China in 2014[clxxii] while the famous *Pretty Woman* actor Richard Gere has received scant offers for blockbuster acting roles since criticizing China's policies towards Tibet. Depp has promoted science fictions movies like *Transcendence,* with a Chinese company, DMG Entertainment, handling distribution in China. In this film, the actor depicts a mad scientist who creates a computer that can upload human consciousness into a new body that merges man with machine, a hint at elite aspirations to achieve immortality through technology.

While NFL football players have "taken a knee" at football games to highlight racial profiling and "resist" the so-called racist Trump Administration, the NFL is making inroads into China, which ruthlessly persecutes minorities and jails dissidents. NFL players have not spoken up against Chinese human rights violations, reflecting that taking a knee is based more upon resisting Trump's anti-globalist agenda than taking a principled stand for human rights. Chinese money is often the incentive.

In 2017, the NFL signed a streaming agreement with China's Internet company Tencent, *Fortune* reported.[clxxiii] According to *NFL News,*[clxxiv] the National Football League sought to celebrate its 100th anniversary by playing a game in China.

In 2008, the NFL announced a digital partnership with Youku, Alibaba Group's video entertainment platform, "to bring high-quality football programming to Chinese fans" that features "weekly programming on Youku's sports channel, including game highlights and behind-the-scenes stories from NFL games such as the Super Bowl, NFL Kickoff, Thanksgiving, and the NFL International series." The partnership includes multi-screen online video sharing and streaming platforms in China.

If San Francisco 49ers superstar Colin Kaepernick had "taken a knee" in China, he would have been thrown in prison. Yet, he eagerly expresses contempt for the United States while the NFL seeks marketing opportunities in a country that is unspeakable brutal to minorities and which does not even consider the rights of its citizens. "I am not going to stand up to show pride in a flag for a country that oppresses black people and people of color," Kaepernick said at a press conference. "To me, this is bigger than football, and it would be selfish on my part to look the other way. There are bodies in the street and people getting paid leave and getting away with murder." When Kaepernick puts his job on the line to take a stand against the "Butchers of Beijing," he may have a leg to stand on.

After Kaepernick "took a knee," he received an endorsement deal from Nike, which posted first-quarter revenues of $1,380,000,000 for business in the Greater China region, boasting in public statements that its relationships with Chinese consumers is "as strong as it can be."[clxxv] After "resisting" Trump, Kaepernick became the face of a Nike advertising campaign, which has received over 80,000,000 views. He has also entertained book deals, speaking tours, and a possible comedy series.[clxxvi] Ironically, the message on Kaepernick's Nike ads reads: "Believe in something even if it means sacrificing everything." Clearly what he believes in is money and self-promotion even if that means sacrificing his dignity, integrity, and patriotism to the United States to become a global superstar. Kaepernick eagerly accepted a lucrative deal to promote a brand that does business in a country that has an abysmal human rights record to "resist" a country whose protections are far greater. Such is the hypocrisy of globalists.

Numerous reports have emerged of Senior Chinese officials encouraging their American counterparts to condemn American trade practices and Trump. For example, China reportedly threatened to deny a business license for a major corporation if its executives criticized China's policies. In order to gain access to China market, American companies are required to partner with Chinese companies and share intellectual property. Once the patents are shared, the American company finds its opportunities in China diminished while the Chinese company goes to create the same product at less cost, with financing from the Communist Chinese government, thereby undercutting the American competition. American joint ventures operating in China are required to establish "party organizations" within their company that give the Chinese Communist Party a voice and veto in hiring and investment decisions.

China has even targeted American voters for propaganda, for example, by paying to have a supplement inserted into the *Des Moines Register* which was designed to look like a news article. The articles portrayed American trade policies as reckless and harmful to Iowans. China Radio International broadcasts Communist-approved programs on 30 outlets in major U.S. cities while its China Global Television network reaches more than 75,000,000 Americans. At the same time, China blocks American news websites within its territory and makes it makes it harder for U.S. journalists to get visas.

Chinese student and scholar associations and so-called Confucius Institutes that established branches across U.S. campuses, enabling hundreds of thousands of Chinese nationals to study in the United States, spread Communist propaganda on U.S. soil, foment dissent, indoctrinate American students, and share U.S. intellectual property with China. At the same time, Chinese women are encouraged to have "anchor babies" in America so that Chinese families can obtain American citizenship and "impair American interests" through the ballot box, as envisioned by Mao.

At the same time, *China Daily*[clxxvii] announced that "No flouting of China's core interests will be tolerated.... Foreign companies should be aware that Chinese people are particularly sensitive to the status of Tibet, Hong Kong, Macao and Taiwan, which are all parts of China. There is not the least reason for Marriott and the other foreign companies to list these regions as independent countries on any occasion.... They should also be aware that they have flouted China's laws, as both the country's Cyber Security Law and the Advertising Law prohibit any individual or company from doing anything that undermines the country's sovereignty and territorial integrity. It goes without saying that any foreign company that makes the mistake of doing so owes the Chinese people a sincere apology, which Marriott and Delta Airlines have both issued. But apart from that, they need to investigate how such terrible mistakes could have been made given the fact they have already been doing business in China for many years and should have known that such actions constitute a violation of China's sovereignty and territorial integrity.... China welcomes all foreign companies to do business in China, and Chinese authorities have reiterated on many occasions China's opening-up policy. But that does not mean foreign enterprises are immune to the consequences of defying China's laws and can flout the core interests of the country." While China demands that Americans respect its sovereignty, the Chinese do not reciprocate.

American money and know are significant factors in China's rise. Now China is attempting to dictate how American companies should conduct themselves and what positions they should adopt as a condition upon which they can access the Chinese market. This is a consequence of Kissinger's valueless foreign policy.

Twitter, Google, YouTube, Yahoo, PayPal, and a host of other tech companies that do business in China have pandered to globalist censorship by de-platforming nationalists, supporters of Trump, and those otherwise critical of China, globalism, communism, or any position that the foreign countries in which these companies do business find objectionable. In turn, American interests and constitutional right to free speech have been eroded.

The Chinese are not inherently evil. They are victims of the same globalist agenda that Americans and other people of the world have endured.[clxxviii] Founding Father Benjamin Franklin whose "legacy had a distinctive place in American culture," looked to the 14 virtues of the *Morals of Confucius* for his scholarship, reflecting the beauty, wisdom, and inspiration of the gentle virtues embraced by the Chinese people before the globalists corrupted their culture just as they have ours. These morals informed his own and those of the founders. Many Jews have also come forward to challenge Zionism on grounds that its practices violate God's laws as enumerated in the *Torah* just as Christians have criticized the Vatican and WCC, which have taken positions that contradict the teachings of the *Bible.*

While Trump has worked hard to ensure that American companies do not relocate overseas, corporations that remain may still not hire American employees, thanks to globalism. To cite an example, in 2017, the Taiwanese electronic firm, Foxconn agreed to build a plant producing LCD panels in Wisconsin, a project that promised to employ as many as 13,000 people and "bring thousands of jobs to the state."

The investment was characterized as "the largest economic development project in the state's history."[clxxix] Wisconsin pledged $3,000,000,000 in tax and performance based incentives, with the local government investing $765,000,000 as long as the company met hiring, wage, and investment targets. While Americans were expecting to be hired, Foxconn entertained the idea of bringing in Chinese personnel to "help staff the large facility ... as it struggles to find engineers and other workers on one of the tightest labor markets in the United."

Oddly, Indians have complained of the same dynamic within their own tribes, that often the executives employed in tribal businesses are not Native and therefore not invested in the preservation of tribal society or protection of the interests of genuine Native tribal members. Rather, the new hires serve the hand that feeds them, enabling elites to have full control of those enterprises

China is poised to erode America's competitive advantage through intellectual property theft and a bottomless pit of revenue. It has sought to collect and manage America's meta-data to further its marketing opportunities and competitive advantage which having access to the minutia and data surrounding American businesses and citizens.

Meanwhile, the Chinese acquisitions of American business continue. In 2014, the Chinese firm Lenovo acquired IBM's server business for $2,300,000,000 in cash and stock.[clxxx] A decade earlier, Lenovo purchased IBM's ThinkPad unit, helping the Chinese firm become the largest personal computer manufacturer in the world. The 2014 deal reflected one of the largest Chinese overseas acquisitions. Google, in turn, is expected to own a 5.94 percent stake in China's Lenovo Group worth $750,000,000 once Lenovo's deal to buy Google's Motorola handset division closes. [clxxxi] The Carlyle Group, which got its start through Alaska Native Corporations, reported in 2014 that it expects China to be its destination for investments.[clxxxii]

The Chinese have also snatched up real estate in the United States, in turn, pricing many Americans out of the market. According to the *Los Angeles Times,* affluent Chinese have driven up the price of housing in suburban Los Angeles, California past the "boom era price...spawning a subset of property brokers and mortgages lenders that cater to their distinct needs and even dictate design details of new subdivisions."[clxxxiii]

San Gabriel Valley, Monterey Park has reportedly been labeled the "first suburban Chinatown." Within San Bernardino and Orange counties and Las Vegas, Chinese immigrants have reportedly sought homes big enough to host lengthy visits from overseas relatives. Chinese buyers bought 12% of all U.S. homes purchased by foreign citizens in 2013, up from 5% in 2007,[clxxxiv] with more than half of those home purchased in California with cash. Americans who have lived in these areas for decades are fleeing the state for more affordable homes.

China also acquired the New York-based Waldorf Hotel, which was established by the famous Astor family, for a cool $2,000,000,000. During his trip to the United Nations in 1974, Chinese Vice Premier Deng Xiaoping stayed at the Waldof-Astoria hotel, the venue in which Secretary of State Henry Kissinger hosted Deng and other Chinese dignitaries. The Anbang Insurance Company, which is run by Deng's son-in-law, plans to restore the building, which is now under Communist Chinese ownership. In a global real estate grab, Anbang has reportedly agreed to pay Hilton Worldwide Holdings $1,950,000,000,000 for one of its towers.

By 2015, China's online transactions topped $540,000,000. By 2020, China's ecommerce market was projected to exceed the combined markets of the United States, Germany, France and Great Britain.[clxxxv] As Alibaba.com founder Jack Ma put it, "In other countries, ecommerce is a way to shop. In China, it's a lifestyle."

According to the *Wall Street Journal,* Google has been working on a version of its Play app store for the Chinese market and has entertained plans to fund $300,000,000 in fiber optic with Chinese carriers partnering with Google to bring faster Internet to Asia. *The Wall Street Journal* relayed that Amazon.com was entering Shanghai's Free Trade Zone to allow retailers to sell more merchandise in China. Its entry into the China market pit the company against Alibaba.

In a country built with American capital and ingenuity, China's largest bank, the ICBC, reportedly holds $2,500,000,000,000 in assets, 70 percent of which is owned by the Communist Chinese government through the CIC, the country's sovereign wealth fund; and Huirij, a government run entity set up to invest in Chinese financial firms. Goldman Sachs holds a stake in ICBC while CIC holds a stake in Morgan Stanley, no doubt accounting for their generous speaking fees to globalist champion Hillary Clinton. As a result of the strategies pursued by globalists, 147 corporations now hold 84 percent of the money in the world, with elites holding a controlling stake in these corporations.[clxxxvi] Yet, even this isn't enough for the select few.

With all the money that stood to be made in China and through globalist-inspired government contracts, can there be any doubt as to why the nation's leading tech firms, Hollywood film studios, NFL teams, news organizations, and multinationals opposed Trump and his nationalist policies while the American people and small businesses supported him?

X.
Trumping the Deep State

When Donald Trump was elected President, the country was seconds before the proverbial strike of midnight. As the hands of the clock inched forward, a new world order was about be ushered in, one led by China with President Hillary Clinton presiding over the collapse of the once great United States. Slowly, but surely, the Deep State had restrained and demoralized the country, not unlike a gang of Lilliputians tying down the giant Gulliver, preventing him from being able to defend himself. The elites had planned this end game over a century ago when they eyed the vast wealth that stood to be made in China. The world was their market place.

As the great American writer Jonathan Steinbeck observed, "the best laid plans of mice and men often go awry." America, having forsaken God, was sliding quickly in the dark abyss of the old world. There was no turning back. Elites who had long planned the destruction and capitulation of the United States were finally witnessing their devilish dream come to fruition. As America began sliding into the darkness, something happened. The people perceived that evil was in their midst, yet felt helpless to change course. Their government no longer answered to them. The media was outright lying. The United States was collapsing through controlled demolition, with the elites knocking out the country's foundation piece by piece. They could not even speak their minds without being called unspeakable names, de-platformed, or viciously retaliated against for the crime of loving their country.

Americans could not fathom how communism had managed to take root in countries around the world. Yet, overnight it had taken root in their own. All they could do is cheer on Trump, whose campaign rallies were overflowing with supporters, whose speeches were electrifying, whose message gave them hope. He spoke the truth that was in their hearts. Finally the American people had a leader who appeared to champion their interests. His words were not the stuff of empty campaign rhetoric. They could feel his sincerity in their hearts. With all the hallmarks of a great leader, Trump was willing to sacrifice his life, his fortune, his business interests, and his reputation for the United States, taking hits personally that his supporters endured in smaller ways. Yet, with each hit, he emerged stronger. He fought back.

He sent the elites into apoplexy. Here was a man would couldn't be bought, who didn't need their money, who didn't care what *they* thought, who was willing and able to stand up for the American people and champion them. He was a God send.

The elites thought so too. Pastor Lindsey Williams said that his elite friends confided in him that Trump was elected because "God intervened." God had heard and answered the prayers of the good American people who knew the fate that awaited them, even if they couldn't articulate it. They desperately wanted a President who would hear and champion them. They prayed and cried out for such a man.

Then, along came Trump. With Trump America has received a period of grace and a second chance, Williams said. The elites could not collapse the economy just yet as Trump would not bail them out. Jobs were coming back. The economy was recovering. He was even making good faith efforts to protect America's borders. He began opening up oil fields to support America's energy independence. Trump curtailed frivolous wars and tried to cut wasteful spending. He also renegotiated free trade agreements, putting America's interests first. He has made it fashionable and acceptable again to speak with reverence towards the Creator, to express love of country, to celebrate the beauty and majesty of religion, to wish our neighbors "Merry Christmas."

America feels like a different place under his leadership. It is beginning to feel like America again. He has been a great champion of the United States and its people, a stark contrast to the previous Administrations and even wannabe President Hillary Clinton who tore the country down every chance she got.

Explaining Trump's rise on a segment of *InfoWars,* Alex Jones said that Trump was recruited by patriots within the Deep State. "People who are part of Delta Force, who are covert action in the Defense Department and CIA, I was contacted from the inside from people who wanted to defeat the globalists, who wanted to bankrupt America," he said on his show. "They were advising Trump on the globalist take over....They wanted to attempt a counter coup against the globalists....Donald Trump was advised by the Special Command Forces out of Florida, the Delta Force, Black Ops in America....They said, 'We need you to rally the troops. We need you to run.' ....They delivered the message, with all the dossiers on what was happening....He was being briefed by top generals....We did what we had to do....We launched a counter coup against them. I'd say 90 percent of the CIA, Defense Intelligence, and Military Special Ops is behind us...There is a war going on in the elite....He was recruited by patriots within the intelligence....In the 1950s, the CIA was trying to make us lose to China, but the Army got pissed and created stay-behind networks in America. China has tens of thousands of front companies. Their propaganda is in every movie you see...Hollywood sold out for Chinese funding....The Communist Chinese have basically run this country since the last 20 years before Trump showed up."

A number of sources have confirmed Jones' characterization, including, for example, former State Department official Steve Pieczenik, who served as Deputy Secretary of State under Henry Kissinger. "The storm was over a year ago when we brought in Trump," he told *InfoWars*. "We in the intelligence community and others helped to bring Trump to the forefront...The storm is over. Hillary (Clinton) is over. (FBI Director Robert) Mueller is over. The FBI is over. The CIA, certain elements, are over. We have several military generals in charge...We have every Congressional district...We have military installments or projects....We in the intelligence and military community are basically in charge. Trump's on top of it."

Pastor Lindsey Williams who first alerted the nation about the non-energy crisis has come forward to affirm that the elite "don't know what to do" now that Trump is in charge. "They are panicking."

In a debate on the Rise of Populism, former *Breitbart* head and Trump campaign adviser Steve Bannon said, "The real reason Donald Trump and the populist movement rose is because of the (George W. Bush) Administration .... On the watch of President Bush, we saw the inexorable rise of China ....We watched the process of the beginning of the de-industrialization of the United States shipping all the manufacturing jobs over there....There is direct correlation between the factories that left and the jobs that went with it and the opioid crisis. It took away people's self worth and dignity. The second is the $7,000,000,000,000 – per Brown University – that's their analysis of the wars that we still haven't won and we're still in 17 years later....That's thousand dead, 40- 50,000 combat casualties and $7,000,000,000,000 spent. Lastly, the financial debacle on their watch.... The populist movement is not racist. Look at the economic benefits that are coming though Trump's policies. They destroyed the Judeo-Christian foundation of society which is the family unit and savings....You can't save any more. You can't have a pension plan...."

This is where globalism has gotten us, with the country now surpassing $22,000,000,000,000 in debt, with the country edging towards totalitarianism and socialism, with the United States being collapsed into a new world order led by Communist China.

This book was written to explain to the public how we got to the point and to spur debate and discussion among the people so that we can eradicate the cancer within America and restore the country. America is great because of its people and values are good, and for those reasons, it can be great again. We are on our way, thanks to President Donald Trump who has provided us that opportunity.

It's up to us as the American people do decide where we go from here, whether we will contribute to our own demise for short termed gain or do what's in the best interests of our country and for our children. First we must educate ourselves and our neighbors. Knowledge is power. By enlightening each other, we can force the dragon out of the shadows.

We must get our fiscal house in order, both nationally and on an individual basis. We can no longer afford to live on debt, nor should the federal government have *carte blanche* to waste the people's money. That there are millionaires, billionaires, and trillionaires, who owe their wealth to little more than crony capitalism while the nation falls to debt speaks to this problem. The United States should not undermine the financial position of its own people and country to leverage that of foreign countries and elites so that they can continue to profit on the public's dime. Perhaps a full audit of the government's finances can be done to track the money and claw it back. Prosecutions should proceed as warranted.

Since the betrayal was coordinated through international networks, patriots within the United States should network with freedom loving people within this country and around the world. The United States should have no qualms about assuming world leadership, one in which it can project its values overseas and within its border, those of freedom, human rights, and rule of law to the world. Values matter. Yet, it should not assume the financial burden for the rest of the world.

The United States should not allow foreign interests, whether Chinese, Israeli, Russian, Arab, or British, to take precedence over our own nor should we all them to interfere in our affairs, curtail our rights, and liberties, or dictate the nation's financial priorities, values, and agenda. We must become a sovereign nation once again, one of, by, and for the people, instead of the world's greatest emerging welfare state and dupe.

Let us use the gifts God has given us to create, rather than to destroy. Together, we can lock hands around the globe to make the world habitable and sustainable for all life upon it for ourselves and future generations as we explore the marvels of science, the edge of the galaxies, and the limitless potential for human ingenuity and progress. With the values and principles enshrined in America's founding documents and ingrained in the hearts of the American people, we can once again be a light unto this dark world.

IX.
The Dragon Speaks

The author Maya Angelou once remarked, "When someone shows you they are, believe them the first time." The following is the actual text of a speech delivered in December, 2005 by Comrade Chi Haotian, the Vice Chairman of China's Military Commission to top officers and generals:

Comrades, I'm very excited today, because the large scale online survey sina.com that was done for us showed that our next generation is quite promising and our Party's cause will be carried on. In answering the question, "Will you shoot at women, children and prisoners of war," more than 80 per cent of the respondents answered in the affirmative, exceeding by far our expectations.

Today I'd like to focus on why we asked sina.com to conduct this online survey among our people. My speech today is a sequel to my speech last time, during which I started with a discussion of the issue of the three islands [Taiwan, Diaoyu Islands and the Spratley Islands] and mentioned that 20 years of the idyllic theme of 'peace and development' had come to an end, and concluded that modernization under the saber is the only option for China's next phase.

I also mentioned we have a vital stake overseas.

The central issue of this survey appears to be whether one should shoot at women, children and

prisoners of war, but its real significance goes far beyond that. Ostensibly, our intention is mainly to figure out what the Chinese people's attitude towards war is: If these future soldiers do not hesitate to kill even noncombatants, they'll naturally be doubly ready and ruthless in killing combatants.

Therefore, the responses to the survey questions may reflect the general attitude people have towards war....

We wanted to know: If China's global development will necessitate massive deaths in enemy countries, will our people endorse that scenario? Will they be for or against it? The fact is, our 'development' refers to the great revitalization of the Chinese nation, which, of course, is not limited to the land we have now but also includes the whole world. As everybody knows, according to the views propagated by the Western scholars, humanity as a whole originated from one single mother in Africa. Therefore no race can claim racial superiority. However, according to the research conducted by most Chinese scholars, the Chinese are different from other races on earth.

We did not originate in Africa.

Instead, we originated independently in the land of China.

Therefore, we can rightfully assert that we are the product of cultural roots of more than a million years, civilization and progress of more than ten thousand years, an ancient nation of five thousand years, and a single Chinese entity of two thousand years. This is the Chinese nation that calls itself 'descendants of Yan and Huang.'

In reviewing history, one may ask: Will the centre of the world civilization shift back to China? Actually, Comrade Liu Huaqing made similar points in early 1980's Based on an historical analysis, he pointed out that the center of world civilization is shifting. It shifted from the East to Western Europe and later to the United States; now it is shifting back to the East. Therefore, if we refer to the 19th Century as the British Century and the 20th century as the American Century, then the 21st Century will be the Chinese Century!!

During our long history, our people have disseminated throughout the Americas and the regions along the Pacific Rim, and they became Indians in the Americas and the East Asian ethnic groups in the South Pacific. We all know that on account of our national superiority, during the thriving and prosperous Tang Dynasty our civilization was at the peak of the world. We were the centre of the world civilization, and no other civilization in the world was comparable to ours.

Later on, because of our complacency, narrow mindedness, and the self enclosure of our own country, we were surpassed by Western civilization, and the centre of the world shifted to the West.

Our Chinese people are wiser than the Germans because, fundamentally, our race is superior to theirs. As a result, we have a longer history, more people, and larger land area. On this basis, our ancestors left us with the two most essential heritages, which are atheism and great unity. It was Confucius, the founder of our Chinese culture, who gave us these heritages. These two heritages determined that we have a stronger ability to survive than the West. That is why the Chinese race has been able to prosper for so long. We are destined 'not to be buried by either heaven or earth' no matter how severe the natural, man-made, and national disasters. This is our advantage.

Take response to war as an example. The reason that the United States remains today is that it has never seen war on its mainland.

Once its enemies aim at the mainland, the enemies would have already reached Washington before its Congress finishes debating and authorizes the president to declare war. But for us, we don't waste time on these trivial things

Maybe you have now come to understand why we recently decided to further promulgate atheism. If we let theology from the West into China and empty us from the inside, if we let all Chinese people listen to God and follow God, who will obediently listen to us and follow us? If the common people don't believe Comrade Hu Jintao is a qualified leader, begin to question his authority, and want to monitor him, if the religious followers in our society question why we are leading God in churches, can our Party continue to rule China??

The first pressing issue facing us is living space. This is the biggest focus of the revitalization of the Chinese race. In my last speech, I said that the fight over basic living resources (including land and ocean) is the source of the vast majority of wars in history. This may change in the information age, but not fundamentally.

Our per capita resources are much less than those of Germany's back then. In addition, economic development in the last twenty-plus years had a negative impact, and climates are rapidly changing for the worse. Our resources are in very short supply. The environment is severely polluted, especially that of soil, water, and air.

Not only our ability to sustain and develop our race, but even its survival is gravely threatened, to a degree much greater than faced Germany back then Anybody who has been to Western countries know that their living space is much better than ours. They have forests alongside the highways, while we hardly have any trees by our streets. Their sky is often blue with white clouds, while our sky is covered with a layer of dark haze. Their tap water is clean enough for drinking, while even our ground water is so polluted that it can't be drunk without filtering. They have few people in the streets, and two or three people can occupy a small residential building; in contrast our streets are always crawling with people, and several people have to share one room. Many years ago, there was a book titled *Yellow Catastrophes*. It said that, due to our following the American style of consumption, our limited resources would no longer support the population and society would collapse once our population reaches 1.3 billion.

Now our population has already exceeded this limit, and we are now relying on imports to sustain our nation. It's not that we haven't paid attention to this issue. The Ministry of Land Resources is specialized in this issue.

But we must understand that the term 'living space' (lebenstraum) is too closely related to Nazi Germany. The reason we don't want to discuss this too openly is to avoid the West's association of us with Nazi Germany, which could in turn reinforce the view that China is a threat. Therefore, in our emphasis on He Xin's new theory, 'Human Rights are just living rights' we only talk about 'living' but not 'space' so as to avoid using the term 'living space.' From the perspective of history, the reason that China is faced with the issue of living space is because Western countries have developed ahead of Eastern countries. Western countries established colonies all around the world, therefore giving themselves an advantage on the issue of living space. To solve this problem, we must lead the Chinese people outside of China, so that they can develop outside of China.

Would the United States allow us to go out to gain new living space? First, if the United States is firm in blocking us, it is hard for us to do anything significant to Taiwan and some other countries!

Second, even if we could snatch some land from Taiwan, Vietnam, India, or even Japan, how much more living space can we get? Very trivial! Only countries like the United States, Canada and Australia have the vast land to serve our need for mass colonization . Therefore, solving the 'issue of America' is the key to solving all other issues. First, this makes it possible for us to have many people migrate there and even establish another China under the same leadership of the CCP.

America was originally discovered by the ancestors of the yellow race, but Columbus gave credit to the White race. We the descendants of the Chinese nation are entitled to the possession of the land!!! It is historical destiny that China and United States will come into unavoidable confrontation on a narrow path and fight. In the long run, the relationship of China and the United States is one of a life and *death struggle.*

Of course, right now it is not the time to openly break up with them yet. Our reform and opening to the outside world still rely on their capital and technology. We still need America. Therefore, we must do everything we can to promote our relationship with America, learn from America in all aspects and use America as an example to reconstruct our country.

Only by using special means to 'clean up' America will we be able to lead the Chinese people there. Only by using nondestructive weapons that can kill many people will we be able to reserve America for ourselves.

There has been rapid development of modern biological technology, and new bio weapons have been invented one after another.

Of course we have not been idle; in the past years we have seized the opportunity to master weapons of this kind. We are capable of achieving our purpose of 'cleaning up' America all of a sudden. When Comrade Xiaoping was still with us, the Party Central Committee had the perspicacity to make the right decision not to develop aircraft carrier groups and focused instead on developing lethal weapons that can eliminate mass populations of the enemy country.

Biological weapons are unprecedented in their ruthlessness, but if the Americans do not die then the Chinese have to die. If the Chinese people are strapped to the present land, a total societal collapse is bound to take place.

According to the computations of the author of Yellow Peril, more than half of the Chinese will die, and that figure would be more than 800 million people! Just after the liberation, our yellow land supported nearly 500 million people, while today the official figure of the population is more than 1.3 billion. This yellow land has reached the limit of its capacity. One day, who know how soon it will come, the great collapse will occur any time and more than half of the population will have to go.

It is indeed brutal to kill one or two hundred million Americans. But that is the only path that will secure a Chinese century, a century in which the CCP leads the world. We, as revolutionary humanitarians, do not want deaths, But if history confronts us with a choice between deaths of Chinese and those of Americans, we'd have to pick the latter, as, for us, it is more important to safeguard the lives of the Chinese people and the life of our Party.

The last problem I want to talk about is of firmly seizing the preparations for military battle. The central committee believes, as long as we resolve the United States problem at one blow, our domestic problems will all be readily solved.

Therefore, our military battle preparation appears to aim at Taiwan, but in fact is aimed at the United States, and the preparation is far beyond the scope of attacking aircraft carriers or satellites. Marxism pointed out that violence is the midwife for the birth of the new society. Therefore war is the midwife for the birth of China's century."

The shadow dragon has spoken. Is America listening?

i   Kaphle, Anup, *Columbia Journalism Review,* March, April 2015.
ii Martin, Justin, "Loneliness at the Foreign Bureau," *Columbia Journalism Review, April 23, 2012.*
iii Kiger, Patrick, "Did Colonists Give Infected Blankets to Native Americans as Biological Warfare?" *History.com*, November 15, 2018. According to the *History Channel,* weaponizing small pockets against Native Americans was first reported by the 19th century historian Francis Parkman, who came across correspondence in which Sir Jeffrey Amherst, commander in chief of the British forces in North American in the 1760s had discussed its use with British Col. Henry Bouquet, a subordinate.
iv Dennett, Charlotte and Colby, Gerald, <u>Thy Will be Done: The Conquest of the Amazon, Nelson Rockefeller, and Evangelism in the Age of Oil.</u>
v   Ibid.
vi Ibid.
vii Ibid.
viii Ibid.
ix Jeff Benedict's book, <u>Without Reservation</u> documents the fraud in the membership rolls of the Mashantucket Pequot tribe. Susan Bradford's <u>Lynched: The Shocking Story of How the Political Establishment Manufactured a Scandal to Have Republican Superlobbyist Jack Abramoff Removed from Power</u> reveals the fraud rife throughout the membership rolls of the Saginaw Chippewa Indian Tribe. Tribal members report that membership fraud is endemic throughout Indian Country.
x   Rumsfeld, Donald, <u>Known and Unknown: A Memoir.</u>
xi Ibid.
xii Wallace-Wells, Benjamin, "Polar Fleeced," *Washington Monthly,* July 1, 2001.
xiii Briody, Dan, <u>The Iron Triangle: Inside the Secret World of the Carlyle Group.</u>
xiv Stine, Laura, "Bad News," *Anchorage Press,* June 30, 2016.
xv Wallace-Wells, Benjamin, "Polar Fleeced," *Washington Monthly,* July 1, 2001.
xvi Enlich, Lisa, <u>Goldman Sachs: The Culture of Success</u> and Beard, Patricia, <u>Blue Blood and Mutiny: Thee Fight for the Soul of Morgan Stanley.</u>
xvii Newman, Bud, "Neil Bush Hit with 'Cease and Desist' Order for S&L Conflict," *UPI,* April 18, 1991.
xviii Source: *The Navajo Times,* May 1, 1975.
xix Gillenkirk, Jeff and Dowie, Mark, "The Great Indian Power Grab: Is Peter MacDonald the Moses of the Navajo Nation, or is He an Energy Baron Out for Himself and a Few Loyal Cronies?" *Mother Jones,* January 1982.
xx Hitchens, Christopher, <u>The Missionary Position: Mother Teresa in Theory and Practice.</u>
xxi Binstein, Michael and Bowden, Charles, <u>Trust Me: Charles Keating and the Missing Billions.</u>
xxii Dennett, Charlotte and Colby, Gerald, <u>Thy Will be Done: The Conquest of the Amazon, Nelson Rockefeller, and Evangelism in the Age of Oil.</u>

xxiii   There remarks were attributed to Richard Monette, the Chairman and COE of the 30,000 member Turtle Mountain Bank of Chippewa Indians.
xxiv   https://www.oddfellows.co.uk/About-us/History
xxv   Turner, Stanfield, Burn Before Reading.
xxvi   Source: National Park Service.
xxvii   Langer, Emily, "Frederick Mayer, German Jew who Returned to Nazi Europe as U.S. Spy, Dies at 94," *Washington Post,* April 26, 2016.
xxviii   Source: National Park Service.
xxix   Turner, Stanfield, Burn Before Reading.
xxx   Ibid.
xxxi   Ibid.
xxxii   Trenton, Joseph, Prelude to Terror.
xxxiii   "Hank Greenberg on China Trade, Starr's Rapid Growth, and 100th, Spitzer, Schneiderman, and More," *Risk & Insurance,* October, 12, 2018.
xxxiv   Rooney, Francis and Negroponte, John, The Global Vatican: An Inside Look at the Catholic Church, World Politics, and Extraordinary Relationship between the United States and Holy See.
xxxv   Hooft, W.A. Visser T., The Genesis and Formation of the World Council of Churches,
xxxvi   Bundy, Edgar, Collectivism in the Churches
xxxvii   Bundy, Edgar, How the Communists Use Religion. Ambassador Francis Rooney, who had served as U.S. Ambassador to the Vatican wrote in The Global Vatican that the National Council of Churches "were in league with the Communists to the point of being a state church with Russian and other communist countries. Russian President Vladimir Putin exerts tremendous influence on the Russian Orthodox church to this day.
xxxviii   Ibid.
xxxix   Porterfield, Amanda, The Transformation of American Religion: The Story of a Late Twentieth Century Awakening,
xl   Colby, Gerard and Dennett, Charlotte, Thy Will Be Done: The Conquest of the Amazon: Nelson Rockefeller and Evangelism in the Age of Oil.
xli   Porterfield, Amanda, The Transformation of American Religion: The Story of a Late Twentieth Century Awakening,
xlii   Colby, Gerard and Dennett, Charlotte, Thy Will Be Done: The Conquest of the Amazon: Nelson Rockefeller and Evangelism in the Age of Oil.
xliii   Federal Council of Churches, Yearbook of the Church and Social Services.
xliv   Hooft, W.A. Visser T., The Genesis and Formation of the World Council of Churches,
xlv   Bundy, Edward, Collectivism in the Churches.
xlvi   *New York Times,* July 30, 1946.
xlvii   Bundy, Edward, Collectivism in the Churches
xlviii   "Riverside Opens Its Doors to Occupy Wall St. Supporters," *Riverside blog*, www.theriversidechurchny.org/news, Nov. 18, 2011.

xlix   Rooney, Francis and Negroponte, John, The Global Vatican: An Inside Look at the Catholic Church, World Politics, and Extraordinary Relationship between the United States and Holy See.
l   Ibid.
li   Ibid.
lii   Alvarez, David, Spies on the Vatican: Espionage and Intrigue from Napoleon to the Holocaust.
liii   Aris, Ben and Campbell, Duncan, "How Bush's Grandfather Helped Hitler's Rise to Power," *Guardian*, September 25, 2004. As the *Guardian* reported, Brown Brothers Harriman served as a U.S..base for the German industrialist, Fritz Thyssen, who had helped finance Hitler's rise in the 1930s, and which profited from Hitler's efforts to reaffirm between the two World Wars. Prescott Bush served as director of the New York-based Union Banking Corporation that represented Thyssen's interests in the United States and continued to support the bank after the United States was enlisted to fight the Nazis and was also reportedly served "on the board of at least one of the companies that formed part of a multinational network of companies to allow Thyssen to move assets around the world." He was also linked to a company that made use of Nazi slave labor from German concentration camps during the war, according to the *Guardian* report.
liv   In The Best Enemy Money Can Buy, Anthony Sutton wrote: "There is no such thing as Soviet technology. Almost all – perhaps 90–95 percent – came directly or indirectly from the United States and its allies. In effect the United States and the NATO countries have built the Soviet Union, its industrial and its military capabilities. This massive construction job has taken 50 years. Since the Revolution in 1917. It has been carried out through trade and the sale of plants, equipment and technical assistance."
lv   "Rockefeller Family Connections with China," *China Daily,* March 21, 2017.
lvi   The Rockefeller Foundation: A Digital History.
lvii   Ibid.
lviii   Ibid.
lix   "Yale Group Spurs Mao's Emergence" and "China Scholars Praise Nixon's Formosa Policy," *Yale Daily News,* No. 96, Feb. 29 1972.
lx   https://divinity.yale.edu/academics/ordination-and-denominational-preparation
lxi   Ibid.
lxii   Rockefeller, "China Traveler, *Time*, 1973.
lxiii   Williams' allegations concerning the crude oil find in Alaska were confirmed by Alan Stang who traveled to Alaska to explore the fields himself and reported his conclusions in *American Opinion*. Also corroborating the find were Secretary of Interior James Watts who appeared in a cover story in the Wall Street Journal affirming that the United States did not have an energy shortage; and Ronald Reagan who said in his Rocky Mountain speech, that there was as much oil in Alaska as in Saudi Arabia.
lxiv   Pastor Lindsey Williams has given numerous presentations, many of which are published online.

lxv   Congressional Record, "Remembering William J. Van Ness," February 7, 2018.
lxvi   Ibid.
lxvii   For example, please see: Kredo, Adam, "Family Close to Saudi Royals Pump Millions into Clinton Foundation, Dem Coffers," *Washington Free Beacon*, May 20, 2016.
lxviii   Baters, Brainerd, "A Peninsula in Profile," *Armaco World*, March/April 1972.
lxix   Eichenwald, Kurt, "Bin Laden Family Liquidates Holdings," *New York Times*, October 26, 2001.
lxx   Posner, Gerald, Secrets of the Kingdom: The Inside Story of the Saudi-U.S. Connection.
lxxi   Including, for example, Joe Ellender and James Russel Barrack.
lxxii   Segev, Tom, "The USSR is Our Second Homeland," Marcy 8, 2013, *Haaretz*.
lxxiii   Weing, David, "The Corporation as Peacemaker," November/December 1997, *Aramco World*
lxxiv   Pieraccini, Federico, "The Untouchable U.S.-Saudi Relationship Element of U.S. Imperialism," Strategic Culture Foundation vis-à-vis *Zero Hedge*.
lxxv   To cite an example, Brazil went to the World Bank for loans. The IMF gave Brazil a line of credit to pay the loans, with Brazil offering the Amazon Basin as credit. When Brazil defaulted on the loans, the World Bank took possession of the Amazon River Basin.
lxxvi   Tracy, William, "Made In," *Armaco World*, January/February, 1977.
lxxvii   Ibid.
lxxviii   Preston, Julia, "Pink Slips at Disney, but First, Training Foreign Replacements," *New York Times*, June 3, 2015.
lxxix   Prins, Nomi, author of Collusion: How Central Banks Rigged the World, made these remarks in a televised interview.
lxxx   Hundreds of millions of federal dollars have been earmarked for tribes and tribal businesses to produce technology for solar energy, biomass, hydrogen, wind, and geothermal industries.
lxxxi   Ben Shelly, Vice President of the Navajo Nation made these remarks at CERT.
lxxxii   Jeremy, Suri, "Henry Kissinger and the American Century," *Executive Intelligence Review*.
lxxxiii   Ibid.
lxxxiv   https://www.sahistory.org.za/people/cecil-john-rhodes
lxxxv   Jeremy, Suri, "Henry Kissinger and the American Century," *Executive Intelligence Review*.
lxxxvi   Ibid.
lxxxvii   Ibid.
lxxxviii   Sutton, Anthony, America's Secret Establishment.
lxxxix   Roberts, Chalmers, "Diplomat David Bruce Dies," *Washington Post*, December 6, 2007.

xc Kissinger Transcripts: The Top Secret Talks with Beijing and Moscow (Edited by William Burr) – transcript dated March of 1973.
xci Kissinger Transcripts: The Top Secret Talks With Beijing And Moscow (Edited by William Burr).
xcii   Ibid.
xciii Ibid.
xciv   Ibid.
xcv   Ibid.
xcvi   Kissinger, Henry, Years of Upheaval.
xcvii This statement was reportedly overheard by a CIA agent and reflects the attitude globalists hold for the United States.
xcviii "Mr. Rhodes' Ideal of Anglo-Saxon Greatness," *New York Times,* April 9, 1902.
xcix   Ibid.
c Buhite, Russell, "Patrick J. Hurley and the Yalta Far Eastern Agreement," *Pacific Historical Review,* Vol 37, Number 3 (August 1969) Buhite was Assistant Professor of History at the University of Oklahoma.
ci Ibid.
cii   The World Economic Forum reported in 2015 that pension funds were underfunded by $70 trillion and that within the United States alone, federal, state, and local government pensions were $7 trillion short. It also reported that Social Security held $50 trillion in unfunded obligation and that corporation pensions were short by $553 billion.
ciii Katz, Yaakov and Bohbot, Amir, "How Israel Used Weapons and Technology to Become an Ally of China," *Newsweek,* May 11, 2017.
civ   Duff, Gordon, "The World if Gore Had Won," *Veteran's Today,* March 18, 2015.
cv "Israel Said to Import $1 Billion in Oil from Iraqi Kurds," *The Times of Israel,* August 24, 2015.
cvi Fulbright delivered these remarks before Congressional hearings on U.S.-China policy in 1966.
cvii   T. William Fulbright's testimony on China-Vietnam before hearings on U.S.-China Policy, 1996.
cviii   *Boston Globe,* November 10, 1940.
cix Smith-Mundt Modernization Act of 2012
cx Bech, Roy, "Ted Kennedy's Immigration Legacy and Why Did He Do It," Numbers USA, September 12, 2009.
cxi Ibid.
cxii   Cohen, Jerome, "Ted Kennedy's Role in Restoring Diplomatic Relations with China," *Public Policy,* Vol. 14:346. Cohen was an Adjunct Senior Fellow for Asia at the Council of Foreign Relations.
cxiii   Buncombe, Andrew, "JFK Was Ready to Use Nuclear Bombs on China, Tapes Reveal," *The Independent,* August 27, 2005.
cxiv   Woodward, Bob and Duffy, Brian, *Washington Post,* January 2, 1997.
cxv   Exec Order 12803 (1992)

cxvi   Soloman, John and Spann, Alison, "Bill Clinton Sought State's Permission to Meet with Russian Nuclear Official During Obama Uranium Decision," *The Hill,* October 19, 2017.

cxvii   Nichols had worked as Marketing Director for the Arkansas Development Finance Authority.[

cxviii   "Aneurism or Arkancide – Larry Nichols Discusses the Untimely Death of Jenny," Larry Nichols Live Stream, August 14, 2018.

cxix   Cobb, Osro, <u>Osro Cobb of Arkansas Memories of Historical Significance</u> and Cobb, Osro, <u>Osro Cobb of Arkansas: Pathways to a Greater Future.</u>

cxx   Timperlake, Edward and Triplett, William, <u>Year of the Rat: How Bill Clinton Compromised U.S. Security for Chinese Cash</u>

cxxi   Schmitt, Erick, "An Unlikely Alliance over China Trade," *New York Times,* May 8, 2020.

cxxii   Timperlake, Edward and Triplett, William, <u>Year of the Rat: How Bill Clinton Compromised U.S. Security for Chinese Cash</u>

cxxiii   *USA Today,* July 15, 2006,

cxxiv   "Foreign Company Now Owns Six Major U.S. Toll Roads," *Truckers Report.*

cxxv   "U.S. Roads, Bridges Being Sold to Foreign Companies," *Associated Press,* July 15, 2006.

cxxvi   Cole, Michael, "NY's Silverstein Properties Bet $2.2 Billion on China Free Trade Zone," *Forbes*, January 28, 2014.

cxxvii   Navrozov, Lev, "Ex-Chinese Official Details Plan for World Domination," *Newsmax*, September 17, 2009.

cxxviii   Collins, Mike, "The Big Bank Bailout," *Forbes*, July 14, 2015.

cxxix   Ellis, Curtis, "Trade Agreement is a Trojan Horse for Obama's Immigration Agenda," *The Hill*, April 13, 2015.

cxxx   Heiderman, Rosalind, "For Hillary Clinton and Boeing: A Beneficial Relationship," *Washington Post,* April 13, 2014.

cxxxi   Source: Public records and transcripts released by the National Committee on United States-China Relations.

cxxxii   Ibid.

cxxxiii   Ibid.

cxxxiv   Source: Public records and transcripts released by the National Committee on United States-China Relations.

cxxxv   *2002 Annual Report, National Committee on United States-China Relations.*

cxxxvi   *2008 Annual Report, National Committee on United States-China Relations.*

cxxxvii   *2009 Annual Report, National Committee on United States-China Relations.*

cxxxviii   Also known as One Belt and One Road and the 21st century Maritime Silk Road which was launched in 2013.

cxxxix   Waters, Clay, "*NYT*'s Thomas Friedman Again Praises Communist China for Getting Things Done," *News Busters,* September 9, 2009.

cxl   So far, China has signed cooperation agreements with at least 40 countries and organizations.

cxli Beijing claims to have exceeded $3,000,000,000,000 between 2014 and 2016, with China's investment in those countries reportedly surpassing $50,000,000,000; it has also established at least 50 economic cooperation zones in at least 20 countries, creating over $1,000,000,000 in revenue.

cxlii The 57 AIIB signatories include Australia, Brazil, Denmark, Georgia, Indonesia, Jordan, Laos, Malta, Netherlands, Pakistan, Qatar, South Africa, Sweden, Turkey, Vietnam, Austria, Brunei, Egypt, Germany, Iran, Kazakhstan, Luxembourg, Mongolia, New Zealand, Philippines, Russia, South Korea, Switzerland, United Arab Emirates, Azerbaijan, Cambodia, Finland, Iceland, Israel, Kuwait, Malaysia, Myanmar, Norway, Poland, Saudi Arabia, Spain, Tajikistan, United Kingdom, Bangladesh, China, France, India, Italy, Kyrgyzstan, Maldives, Nepal, Oman, Portugal, Singapore, Sri Lanka, Thailand, and Uzbekistan.

cxliii A Special Declaration of the Belt and Road was signed during the Second China-CELAC Ministerial Forum in January 2018 which offered "a new platform for mutually beneficial cooperation" between China and Latin America, with invitations extended to Latin American and Caribbean countries. China has also formally incorporated individual Latin American countries into BRI though bilateral Belt and Road Cooperation Agreements. As of June 2018, roughly 70 countries had signed these agreements within Latin America, the first being Panama.

cxliv Vozzella, Laura and Denyer, Simon, "Donor to Clinton Foundation, McAuliffe Caught up in Chinese Cash-for-Votes Scandal," *Washington Post*, September 16, 2016.

cxlv Xinhua, "World Bank Prepared to Provide for BRI Projects," *Xinhua*, November 1, 2011.

cxlvi "One Belt, One Road – And Many Questions," *Financial Times*, May 14, 2017.

cxlvii China Railway 21 Bureau Group Company signed to upgrade the 79.1-km Jimma-Agaro-Didessa road, China State Construction Engineering Corporation agreed to construct two networks along the 84.2-km Mesel/Musle-Kora/Kori-Teru road, and China Communications Construction Company signed to construct the 53.5-km Arsi Robe-Agarfa Ali road and the 53.08-km Mekaneyesus/Este-Simada-Saint road.

cxlviii These examples were provided by the RWR Advisory Group.

cxlix Harel, Amos, *Haaretz*, September 17, 2018.

cl Ehrlich, Richard, "China Getting Too Close To Israel?" *Asia Times*, December 23, 2018.

cli Harel, Amos, "Amid Trump Pressure, Israel Mulls Cooling Burgeoning China Ties: American Concerns of Chinese Technology in Israel a Central Focus of Bolton's Jerusalem Meetings, as Defense Officials Worry that Beijing Might Use Products to Collect Intelligence," *Haaretz*, January 7, 2019.

clii Gordon, Dave, "Unlikely Partners? China and Israel Deepening Trade Ties," BBC, July 19, 2018.

cliii   Katz, Yaakov and Bohbot, Amir, "How Israel Used Weapons and Technology to Become an Ally of China," *Newsweek*, May 11, 2017.
cliv   Katz, Yaakov and Bohbot, Amir, "How Israel Used Weapons and Technology to Become an Ally of China," *Newsweek*, May 11, 2017.
clv Rosenberg, David, "Israel Will Have to Choose between American and China: America's Emerging Pressure on Israel to Cool its Love Affair with China May Not Have Such Terrible Consequences," *Haaretz*, January 8, 2019.
clvi   Nagen, , Yakov, "China Discovers Talmud and the Kabbalah," *Times of Israel,* December 26, 2017.
clvii   Fish, Isaac Stone, "In China, Pushing the Talmud as a Business Guide," *Newsweek*, December 29, 2010.
clviii   Durden, Tyler, "New U.S. Intelligence Study: China 'Already Leads the World' in Key Weapons Technologies," *Zero edge*, January 17, 2019. The DIA report is entitled *China's Military Power.*
clix   Charlie Rose interview with James Clapper, June 25, 2011
clx   Durden, Tyler, "China Hacked IBM and HP, Then Went After Their Clients," *Zero Hedge,* December 20, 2018.
clxi   Whitehead, John, "The Twelve Rules Of Christmas (A Constitutional Q&A)," The Rutherford Institute.
clxii   DeTocqueville, Alexis, <u>Democracy in America</u>.
clxiii   Rogin, Josh, " Lawmakers Demand Answers on AP's Relationship with Chinese State Media," *Washington Post,* December 24, 2018.
clxiv   Her father is Mei Yi.
clxv   Nelson, Christina, "Inside China's Media Revolution," *China Business Review,* March 20, 2014.
clxvi   Qin, Amy and Carlsen, Audrey, "How China Controls Hollywood Scripts," The Central Tibetan Administration, November 19, 2018.
clxvii   Ibid.
clxviii   Ibid.
clxix   Swanon, Ana, "China's Influence Over Hollywood Grows," *Washington Post,* September 24, 2016.
clxx   Swanson, Ana, "Stephen Colbert's 'Pander Express' is a Brilliant Takedown of How Hollywood Sucks up to China," *Washington Post,* October 10, 2015.
clxxi   Peters, Chris, "Walt Disney, Shanghai Media Group to Develop Disney-branded Movies," Reuters, Walt Disney, Shanghai Media Group to develop Disney-Branded movies, March 6, 2014.
clxxii   Coonan, Clifford, "Johnny Depp Makes First Trip to China," *Hollywood Reporter*, March 31, 2014.
clxxiii   Detrick, Hallie, "Hollywood Is Having Trouble in China—But Not for the Reason You'd Think," *Fortune*, May 28, 2018.
clxxiv   Patra, Kevin, "NFL Aiming to Potentially Play Game in China in 2019," *NFL News,* June 30, 2017.
clxxv   Jiang, Ethel, " NIKE: Business is Booming in China," *Business Insider,* September 26, 2018.
clxxvi   Creswell, Julie, Draper, Kevin, and Maheshwari, Sapna, "Nike Nearly

Dropped Colin Kaepernick Before Embracing Him," New York Times, September 26, 2018.

clxxvii "No Flouting of China's Core Interests Will be Tolerated," *China Daily*, January 14, 2018.

clxxviii Wang, David, "Benjamin Franklin and Chinese Civilization," St. Johns University, September 5, 2007.

clxxix Durden, Tyler, "Foxconn May Bring Chinese Workers to its New Wisconsin Facility," *Zero Hedge,* November 6, 2018.

clxxx Kharpal, Arjun, "Lenovo to Buy IBM's Low End Server Business for $2.3 Billion," CNBC, January 23, 2014.

clxxxi "Google to Own $750 Million Lenovo Stake After Motorola Deal Closes; HK Exchange," Reuters, February 6, 2014.

clxxxii Koons, Cynthia, "Carlyle Targets China, Health Care, Consumer, and Food Industries," *Wall Street Journal,* March 24, 2014.

clxxxiii Sreckard, Scott and Khouri, Andrew, "Wealthy Chinese Home Buyers Boost Suburban L.A. Housing Markets," *Los Angeles Times,* March 24, 2014.

clxxxiv National Assn. of Realtors.

clxxxv Alibaba Group Research Center.

clxxxvi Upbin, Bruce, "The 147 Companies That Control Everything," *Forbes*, October 22, 2011.

Made in the USA
Monee, IL
13 May 2021